SUKKOS

A SYMPHONY OF JOY

MOSAICA PRESS

SUKKOS

A SYMPHONY OF JOY

RABBI IMMANUEL BERNSTEIN

Mosaica Press, with its team of acclaimed editors and designers, is attracting some of the most compelling thinkers and teachers in the Jewish community today. Our books are impacting and engaging readers from around the world.

ISBN: 978-1-961602-08-3

Published by Mosaica Press, Inc.
www.mosaicapress.com
info@mosaicapress.com

לעילוי נשמת

יעקב בן שלמה צבי הלוי

רחל בת מאיר

יעקב בן זכריה

אוגסתה בת דוד

נחום שלמה בן יוסף

פנינה בת משה

רונלד בן ג'וליאן

מארגו בת סתנלי

ת.נ.צ.ב.ה.

In recognition of the revelation of the *ohr ganuz*
within these pages and the pages
of all of Rav Immanuel Bernstein's *sefarim*.

Dedicated in the merit of our parents

SIMON AND BARRIE JACOB

STEVEN AND YVETTE FISHBEIN

May they live long and meaningful lives filled with *nachat*.

And in the merit of our children

SHLOMO HILLEL, ELEAYA LEORA,
NESSIA TSOFIA, CHARLOTTE CHANA,
YOSEPH AZARIAH, NOAH BINYAMIN,
EPHRAIM RAHAMIM, AND ASHER EMANUEL

May they find satisfaction and success
in their learning, *shidduchim*, and life.

With unending gratitude,
OVADIAH AND LEILA JACOB

In loving memory of

STELLA BAT BINYAMIN

HARRIET BAT YEHUDA

Sukkos is the holiday of *simchah*. These two women constantly inspired us with their joy and approach to life. We are still learning from them daily, aiming to apply even a fraction of their *simchas hachayim* to our days. A sukkah envelops anyone inside it, becoming a nurturing hug from Hashem and a home away from home. These women embodied those characteristics. They were a warm hug, a kind face. They were home to us. May the learning from this book be a merit for their beautiful *neshamos*.

THE SEGAL FAMILY

Dedicated in loving memory of our
parents and grandparents

ISADORE AND BELLE GLASTEIN
ISAAC AND FRIEDA SUTTON

ר' יחזקאל ב"ר יעקב דוב ז"ל | מרת בילא בת ר' בנימין ע"ה
ר' יצחק ב"ר יוסף ז"ל | מרת פרידא בת ר' יוסף ע"ה

With love,
DR. CARY AND DEBORAH GLASTEIN
IAN AND SOPHIE GLASTEIN
ZACK AND RITA CARLA GLASTEIN

Dedicated in loving memory of

DOVID BEN SHIMSHON, ZT"L

Who survived the Shoah and who we know
would be so proud of his great-grandchildren,
whose lives embody the eternal heritage for which
he and others sacrificed so much.

With love and gratitude,
ADAM AND CHANI SAUNDERS

Dedicated in loving memory of our dear grandparents

יעקב נח בן מרדכי | חיה שיינדל בת יצחק

משה בן דב בער | חיה שרה בת שמואל

אברהם צבי בן חיים | דייל בת עדווארד

יעקב בן אהרן איטל | גיטל בת רב מנחם מנדל

With love,
EZRA AND SHIRA GALSTON

In memory of our grandparents
and great-grandparents

נתן ושרה הריס ע"ה

Who instilled in us
a passion for and pride in being a Jew
a deep love for the Jewish People
and a sense of responsibility and kindness
toward our fellow man.

With love and affection,
שמואל ואילנה הריס ומשפחתם

אַשר זעליג וייס

כגן 8

פעיה"ק ירושלם ת"ו

בס"ד

ח' תמוז תשפ"ג

This *sefer*, authored by my dear friend, Rabbi Immanuel Bernstein, on the topic of the festival of Sukkos, is an outstanding work. In it, the author brings together ideas from Chazal and the Torah luminaries over the generations, examining the festival of Sukkos, its mitzvos and its customs. The *sefer* is overflowing with insight and gives the reader the opportunity to attain a new and deeper connection with the holy days of Sukkos.

Many have benefited greatly from Rabbi Bernstein's earlier *sefarim*, which are both fascinating and original, and I have no doubt that they will from this one as well. My blessing to my dear friend, Rabbi Bernstein, *shlita*, is that he may merit to continue spreading the greatness and glory of Torah in joy and tranquility.

In friendship and blessing,

תפארת גדליה

YGW

From the Desk of

RABBI AHRON LOPIANSKY

Rosh HaYeshiva

Tammuz 5783

"And Moshe declared the appointed _moadim_ to the children of Israel (Vayikra 29:43). From here we derive that it is obligatory to read on each holiday, its portion in the Torah (Megillah 32a)."

One may read this _passuk,_ with some homiletical license, to mean that through Moshe's teachings, he caused the _moadim_ to "speak". Every _moed_ is marked by many _mitzvos_ that are the basis for **experiencing** the special kedusha associated with that _zman._ But only when we engage in the Torah study of these _moadim,_ do the _moadim_ **speak** to us. It is thus critical to study about each Yomtov in under to gain the full appreciation of it.

Rabbi Bernstein has written a wonderful _sefer_ in line with this guidance. He has taken the _moed_ of _simcha, succos,_ and at length discusses all aspects of it, until we gain an overarching sense of the broader meaning of this Yom Tov.

It is my _bracha_ that he continues enhancing our _zmanim,_ with more of such comprehensive and sweeping discussions, of their meanings and content.

Ahron Shraga Lopiansky

TABLE OF CONTENTS

SECTION A
THE FESTIVAL OF SUKKOS

Introduction—And a Question / Pesach, Shavuos, and Sukkos—An Unusual Partnership / The Message of the Ananei Hakavod / The Timing of the Festival / The Disappearance—And Return—Of the Ananei Hakavod / Clouds That Surround and Clouds That Guide / The Mishkan and the Ananei Hakavod—Inside and Out / From the Mishkan to the Sukkah / The Arba Minim—Four That Are One

Introduction: In the Prayers—And in the Verses / Baalei HaTosafos—Stages in the Harvest / Between Clouds and Huts / Two Tracks of Yom Tov / Sukkos—A Double Yom Tov / Completing the Process

In the Rishonim: The Abarbanel and the Rambam / Yehoshua and Ezra: Two Special Sukkos Celebrations / Hoshanos and the Walls of Jericho / The Ananei Hakavod and the Land of Israel / Ananei Hakavod and the Gathering of the Harvest

Joy / Peace

SECTION C
SUKKOS IN THE BEIS HAMIKDASH

SECTION D
THE CONCLUDING DAYS OF SUKKOS

ACKNOWLEDGMENTS

I would like to express my thanks to all those who reviewed the manuscript of this *sefer*. A special thank you to my dear *talmidim*, Shmuel Levenson and Marc Osian, for their thorough review and extremely helpful and insightful comments.

My thanks to Zev and Rena Lewis for their continued encouragement and support in all my writing projects.

I would like to thank Rabbis Yaacov Haber and Doron Kornbluth of Mosaica Press for overseeing this project, Rabbi Kornbluth for once again bringing his consummate editing skills to the manuscript, and to the entire Mosaica team for their trademark excellence in producing the *sefer*.

This *sefer* was dedicated by my dear friend Mr. Avi Weinstock in memory of his father, R' Yisroel, *z"l*. It is my hope that the words of Torah contained within will be an *iluy* for his *neshamah* and an honor for his memory.

I would like to take this opportunity to pay special tribute to my dear *rebbi*, Rabbi Chaim Walkin, *zt"l*, who passed away in Cheshvan of this past year. A scion of an illustrious rabbinic family, he embodied the wisdom and nobility of the rich Lithuanian legacy to which he was heir— a *mesorah* he graciously and generously shared with all those whom he felt it could enrich, uplift, and inspire.

His impact on me in my formative years in Yeshivas Ateres Yisrael, where he served as the *mashgiach ruchani*, was decisive and transformational. Indeed, he gave of his entire self to each and every *talmid*, to the extent that hundreds of people were for years fully convinced that he had no other *talmidim* like them—that is, until they met each other and shared their recollections at the *levayah* and the shivah. Only then did a glimpse of the magnitude of his impact and influence begin to emerge.

Beyond these special relationships with *talmidim*, he spread goodness and encouragement wherever he went, often to people he did not know and would meet only once, but who were all moved and uplifted by the love that they could feel exuded from his quintessential Jewish heart.

It is appropriate to recall at the beginning of a *sefer* on Sukkos that the last time I was privileged to see him was in his sukkah on Chol Hamoed of this past Sukkos, just a few weeks before he passed away. Though it was hard for him to move, he was still able to share some *divrei Torah* of which he was particularly fond, embellished with one or two light comments and accompanied by his priceless smile and the twinkle of his eyes. May his memory be a blessing, and may the beauty of his ways serve as an example and inspiration for generations to come.

As with every *sefer* I have written—and probably everything else of worth I have done in the last two and a half decades—the ability to write this *sefer* was due to my dear wife, Judy, who allowed me to focus singularly on this project and give it the time, attention, and energy it required. May we continue to share *nachas* from our children, and *baruch Hashem*, more recently, grandchildren, in good health and with gladness of heart.

I.B.

Jerusalem, 5783

INTRODUCTION

Of all the festivals of the Torah, Sukkos is arguably the most elusive.

On the one hand, we refer to it as *zman simchaseinu*—the time of our joy, marking it as the quintessential time of celebration. Yet on the other hand, it is not clear what exactly we are celebrating. The reason given by the Torah itself, that Hashem made us dwell in huts in the wilderness, risks making us even more confused. How is that cause for celebration?

The mitzvos of the festival are likewise enigmatic. What lies behind the many specifications regarding how a sukkah must be made? What is the meaning of the four species we take, wave in all directions, and circle the *bimah* while holding? What is the reason for the special water libation in the Beis Hamikdash during Sukkos, and why was it accompanied by such great festivity? Additionally, where does Shemini Atzeres fit in with all of this? Is it the final day of Sukkos or perhaps a separate Yom Tov? If so, what does it celebrate? And what about Hoshana Rabbah?

Each of the above mitzvos requires our contemplation, and more still is demanded when considering how they all come together around the essential theme or themes of the festival.

This book is dedicated to answering these questions. Drawing on a broad range of classical sources from across the generations, it provides the reader with new insight into how all the above elements come together to form the symphony of Sukkos.[1] The ideas contained within these chapters should hopefully serve to deepen our appreciation of the festival, enhance our performance of its mitzvos and customs, and elevate our feeling of joy during this special time.

May we merit to connect with the holy days of Sukkos and Shemini Atzeres, may the joy of this festival pour forth into the year ahead, and may this all bring us a decisive step closer to celebrating once again in the Beis Hamikdash, speedily in our days.

---

1   My earlier *sefer*, *Teshuvah*, ended with a section on Sukkos as the culmination of the *Yamim Noraim*. Many of those ideas have been incorporated and expanded upon in this *sefer*.

THE FESTIVAL
OF SUKKOS

CHAPTER 1

WHAT DOES SUKKOS COMMEMORATE?

INTRODUCTION–AND A QUESTION

The mitzvah of sukkah is distinguished among mitzvos in that the Torah itself provides the reason for the mitzvah:

למען ידעו דרתיכם כי בסכות הושבתי את בני ישראל בהוציאי אותם מארץ מצרים:

So that your generations will know that I caused the Children of Israel to dwell in sukkos when I took them out of Egypt.[1]

According to Rabbi Eliezer, the "sukkos" to which the verse refers are the *Ananei Hakavod* (Clouds of Glory) with which Hashem surrounded the Bnei Yisrael during their travels in the *midbar* (wilderness).[2] Many commentators have raised a simple question regarding this idea: The *Ananei Hakavod* were not the only miraculous entity that Hashem provided for Bnei Yisrael in the *midbar*. He caused manna to fall every day

---

1   *Vayikra* 23:43.
2   See *Sukkah* 11b. This is the view that is cited by the *Tur* and *Shulchan Aruch* in the beginning of *Hilchos Sukkah*, *Orach Chaim* 625. According to Rabbi Akiva (*Sukkah* ibid.), the sukkah commemorates actual huts that we dwelled in, see next chapter for a discussion of this dispute.

from the heavens and had a well follow them on their travels to provide them with water. Yet we do not find any festival commemorating those miracles. Why are the *Ananei Hakavod* the only item deemed worthy of being marked by a festival?

PESACH, SHAVUOS, AND SUKKOS—AN UNUSUAL PARTNERSHIP

In truth, there is a more basic question to be raised when considering the festival of Sukkos alongside the other two *Regalim* (pilgrimage festivals), Pesach and Shavuos:

Pesach and Shavuos both commemorate milestone *events* in our becoming a people—Pesach marks the Exodus from Egypt, and Shavuos marks the Giving of the Torah. In contrast to this, Sukkos does not commemorate an event, but rather an *ongoing phenomenon* that lasted decades. How is it then part of the group of three festivals?

THE MESSAGE OF THE ANANEI HAKAVOD

The commentators explain that Sukkos represents the state toward which the other events were destined to bring us. The goal of the Exodus, as well as that of receiving the Torah, was to enable Bnei Yisrael to become Hashem's people. The *Ananei Hakavod* mark the full attainment of that relationship, as they reflect the special protection and closeness that Hashem bestowed upon us as His people. Indeed, the term "glory" in Tanach is a reference to the Divine Presence.[3] Hence, the "Clouds of Glory" are the clouds that demonstrate Hashem's Presence among His people. Moreover, in many places throughout the Chumash and Tanach, Hashem is described as appearing "in a cloud."[4] Therefore, surrounding Bnei Yisrael specifically with clouds represented Hashem, so to speak, bringing the Jewish People into His abode.[5]

We now understand why there is no festival commemorating the manna or the well, even though they were no less miraculous than

---

3   See Rabbeinu Bachya to *Shemos* 24:16.
4   See, for example, *Shemos* 34:5, 40:34.
5   R' Leib Mintzberg, *Ben Melech*, *Sukkos*, p. 17. (See also *Rashi* to *Shir Hashirim* 1:4, "The King brought me into His chambers—these are the Clouds of Glory.")

the *Ananei Hakavod*. The goal of the festival is not to commemorate a miracle per se, but rather to highlight the closeness between Hashem and His people. We fulfill this through dwelling in the sukkah, under the shade of the *schach*. The verse in *Tehillim* describes Hashem's special protection of the Jewish People as follows: "שמרך ה' צלך ה'—Hashem is your Guardian, Hashem is your Shade."[6] Thus, we sit in the sukkah and celebrate the unique relationship we have with Hashem whereby we are His people—and He is our Shade.

Indeed, the very fact that we mark these clouds with a festival every year means that, by definition, there is something about them that affects us every year; for simply to remember a miracle that occurred in the past wouldn't result in an ongoing festival. Thus, for example, the event of the Exodus from Egypt initiated and established our spiritual liberty and identity, the ongoing existence of which we celebrate each year on Pesach. Likewise, the event of receiving the Torah is celebrated on Shavuos each year because it directs and guides our lives every year from that point. So too, the special close relationship with Hashem represented by the *Ananei Hakavod* is commemorated every year because we continue to have that relationship, even as we have moved from actual *Ananei Hakavod* to Hashem's guidance of and supervision over us throughout our history.

THE TIMING OF THE FESTIVAL

With this understanding of the festival, we will be able to answer one of the most famous questions asked regarding Sukkos, as discussed in the *Tur*:[7] Why is Sukkos in Tishrei?

If the goal of Sukkos is to commemorate the *Ananei Hakavod* that accompanied us in the *midbar*, that is something that we received immediately upon leaving Egypt.[8] If so, then it would seem more correct to celebrate Sukkos in Nissan! Not only do we not do this, but the Torah

---

6   121:5.

7   *Orach Chaim* 625.

8   See *Targum Yonasan ben Uziel* to *Shemos* 12:37, commenting on the verse describing the first of the travels of the Jewish People upon leaving Egypt: "From Ramses to Sukkos."

places the festival at the *polar opposite* of the year—exactly six months away, in the middle of Tishrei!

The *Tur* himself responds that since it is usual for people to make huts in the springtime, it would not be apparent that we are doing so in fulfillment of a mitzvah. Therefore, the Torah placed the festival specifically at a time when it is beginning to get cooler and people are actually coming *in* from their summer huts back to the house. To start to make a sukkah at that time makes it clear that it is being done in the performance of a mitzvah.

This answer is most remarkable. According to the *Tur*, the Torah ordained the festival at a point in the year that is not really its intuitively "correct" time so that the intention when making the sukkah should be clearly for the sake of the mitzvah and not confused with some other more practical and seasonal motivation. How does clarity of intent override the consideration of the timing of the festival itself?

Seemingly, the importance that it be clear that we are dwelling in sukkos in fulfillment of a mitzvah also derives from the fact that the Torah provides the goal of the mitzvah as remembering the sukkos in the *midbar*. As such, it is important that the person himself who is doing the mitzvah maintains focus on the sukkah as being commemorative, and not relate to the sukkah simply as a place to be when the weather is warm.

THE DISAPPEARANCE–AND RETURN–OF THE ANANEI HAKAVOD

A classic answer to the *Tur*'s question regarding the timing of Sukkos is provided by the *Vilna Gaon*. He explains that although we received the clouds immediately upon leaving Egypt, we subsequently lost them as a result of the *Cheit Ha'eigel* (Sin of the Golden Calf). As part of the atonement we received on Yom Kippur, the clouds returned to stay with us, and it is this return that we celebrate on the fifteenth of Tishrei—for that is when they returned.[9]

---

9   Commentary to *Shir Hashirim* 1:4.

How is this so?

- Moshe returned from Har Sinai on the day after Yom Kippur, the eleventh of Tishrei, and told the people of Israel to build the *Mishkan*.[10]
- The verse describes them bringing donations of materials for the *Mishkan* "*baboker baboker*," which literally translates as "in the morning, in the morning." The *Vilna Gaon* explains this to mean "on the following two mornings," i.e., the twelfth and the thirteenth.[11]
- On the next day, the fourteenth, they announced that they had enough materials to make the *Mishkan*.
- On the fifteenth, they began building.

At this point, on this day of the fifteenth of Tishrei, the *Ananei Hakavod* returned, signifying the resumption of the special intimate relationship between us and Hashem. This is why we celebrate Sukkos in Tishrei, for we are commemorating the *Ananei Hakavod*—not when we originally got them, but when we got them back![12]

Yet even after the *Vilna Gaon*'s answer, we may persist and ask, Why do we commemorate receiving the *Ananei Hakavod* for the second time and not the first? Surely, as miracles go, they were both equally miraculous, so why wait?

However, when we appreciate that we commemorate the *Ananei Hakavod* not as a miracle per se, but as an expression of our relationship with Hashem, there is infinitely more reason to commemorate their return, for this highlights an entirely new dimension within the relationship, namely, not only is it special, but it is also enduring. Even if we, God forbid, lose the clouds, we can reclaim them. Hence, it is the month of Tishrei, the time when the clouds were restored to us, that contains the festival of Sukkos.

---

10   See *Rashi* to *Shemos* 35:1.

11   *Shemos* 36:3.

12   This explanation is also found in the *Drashos* of *Maharam Chaviv* (*Parshas Emor, drush* 2), citing the earlier work, *Livnas Hasapir*.

In the Prayers: Veratzisa Banu

The special section in the *Amidah* for the festivals begins with the following words:

אתה בחרתנו מכל העמים אהבת אותנו ורצית בנו.

You chose us from among all the nations, You loved us and You desired us.

The commentary *Siach Yitzchak* explains that these three terms refer to the three *Regalim* respectively:

"You chose us from among the nations"—at the time of the Exodus on Pesach.

"You loved us"—as expressed by drawing us close to You at Har Sinai on Shavuos and giving us the Torah.

"And You desired us"—the word *veratzisa* relates not only to the word *ratzon*, "desire," but also to the term *ritzuy*, which means "appeasement." Here, too, although Hashem had removed the *Ananei Hakavod* at the time of the *Eigel Hazahav*, He was subsequently appeased and desired us once more, as celebrated on Sukkos.

CLOUDS THAT SURROUND AND CLOUDS THAT GUIDE

There is an additional element here. The *Vilna Gaon* has stated that when the Jewish People made the *Eigel Hazahav*, the *Ananei Hakavod* departed from them, and this idea can also be found in the *Targum* to *Shir Hashirim*.[13] However, it should be noted that there is a verse which seems to clearly indicate the contrary, for in *Sefer Nechemyah* it states explicitly:

אַף כִּי עָשׂוּ לָהֶם עֵגֶל מַסֵּכָה וַיֹּאמְרוּ זֶה אֱלֹהֶיךָ אֲשֶׁר הֶעֶלְךָ מִמִּצְרָיִם...וְאַתָּה בְּרַחֲמֶיךָ הָרַבִּים לֹא עֲזַבְתָּם בַּמִּדְבָּר אֶת עַמּוּד הֶעָנָן לֹא סָר מֵעֲלֵיהֶם בְּיוֹמָם לְהַנְחֹתָם בְּהַדֶּרֶךְ:

*Even though they made the graven calf and said, "This is your god, Israel, who took you out of Egypt"...You in Your great mercy did not abandon them in the wilderness, **the pillar of cloud did not depart from them by day** to lead them on the way.*[14]

---

13   2:17.
14   9:18–19.

How can the words of the *Vilna Gaon* be resolved in light of this verse?

A very straightforward response adopted by some commentators is that the when the verse in *Nechemyah* says that the cloud did not depart, it refers specifically to the cloud that *went before them*, as the verse itself specifies, "The pillar of cloud did not depart from them by day to lead them on the way." By contrast, the *Vilna Gaon*, who says that the clouds departed when they made the *Eigel Hazahav*, is referring to the other clouds that *surrounded them* on all sides.[15]

The implications of this idea are most profound. As we have seen, the *Ananei Hakavod* represent Hashem's unique relationship with the Jewish People. As such, even when they sinned with the *Eigel Hazahav* and forfeited the *full* relationship—as expressed by the clouds that surrounded them disappearing—nevertheless, the *fundamental* relationship, expressed by the pillar of cloud that guided them, remained. This tells us that not only is our full relationship with Hashem ultimately reclaimable, but our essential relationship with Him is unbreakable—even temporarily! Indeed, in this regard, we could say that it was the fact that the clouds never completely departed that allowed for them to fully return.

Sukkos and Yaakov

The *Tur*, in a well-known passage, draws a parallel between the three *Regalim* and the three patriarchs, respectively.[16] Pesach corresponds to Avraham, Shavuos to Yitzchak, and Sukkos to Yaakov. Indeed, as the *Tur* points out, the first mention of Sukkos in the Torah is actually in connection with Yaakov, as the verse states, "ויעקב נסע סכתה—And Yaakov journeyed to Sukkos."[17]

What is the nature of the connection between Yaakov and the festival of Sukkos?

---

15 See, for example, responsa *Tzitz Eliezer*, vol. 15, sec. 64, and R' Chaim Kanievsky, *Taama D'Kra* to *Nechemyah* loc. cit.

16 *Orach Chaim* 417.

17 *Bereishis* 33:17.

As we have seen, Sukkos celebrates the special and unbreakable connection between Hashem and the Jewish People. This connection is expressed in the verse in *Parshas Haazinu*, "כי חלק ה' עמו יעקב חבל נחלתו‎—For Hashem's portion is His people, Yaakov is the measure of his inheritance."[18] Here, too, we see specific mention of Yaakov within the context of Hashem's unique connection to the Jewish People. What is behind all this?

In truth, historically, we see that Yaakov ushered in a strength of connection between his family and Hashem that did not exist prior to his time. Not all of Avraham's children stayed within his religious program, nor did all those of Yitzchak—for Avraham also had Yishmael, and Yitzchak had Eisav, both of whom left the fold. When it came to Yaakov, however, all his progeny remained within the program. The commentators point out that this is not meant to indicate a superiority of Yaakov over Avraham and Yitzchak. Rather, it was the culmination of a refining process that began with Avraham, continued with Yitzchak, and reached its completion with Yaakov.

The verse cited above regarding the Jewish People being Hashem's portion ends with the words "יעקב חבל נחלתו‎." Although the word "*chevel*" in this context is translated as "measure," it literally means a "rope."[19] Indeed, commenting on the above phrase, *Rashi* writes:

> והוא השלישי באבות המשולש בשלש זכיות, זכות אבי אביו וזכות אביו
> וזכותו, הרי שלשה כחבל הזה שהוא עשוי שלשה גדילים.

> He [Yaakov] is the third of the patriarchs, who has threefold merit: the merit of his grandfather [Avraham], of his father [Yitzchak], and of himself, behold there are three, like a rope that is made from [braiding] three strings.

We can now appreciate the special relationship of Yaakov with Sukkos, as the connection between the Jewish People and Hashem, which Sukkos celebrates, reached completion through Yaakov.

---

18   *Devarim* 32:9. This verse is recited as part of the invitation to the *Ushpizin* on Sukkos.
19   It comes to denote a portion because areas of inheritance were typically measured out using ropes of standard lengths.

THE MISHKAN AND THE ANANEI HAKAVOD—INSIDE AND OUT

We can now further understand why the *Ananei Hakavod* returned to the Jewish People specifically on the day they began to build the *Mishkan*. After all, they had received atonement for the *Cheit Ha'eigel* five days earlier, on Yom Kippur. Why did the clouds return only now?

The purpose of the *Mishkan* is expressed within Hashem's command to build it:

וְעָשׂוּ לִי מִקְדָּשׁ וְשָׁכַנְתִּי בְּתוֹכָם:

They shall make for Me a Mishkan, and I shall dwell in their midst.[20]

As such, the *Ananei Hakavod*, representing Hashem's Divine connection with and supervision of the Jewish People, came back *to surround them* specifically on the day when the people began to make the *Mishkan*—whose purpose is to house the Divine Presence *among them*.

FROM THE MISHKAN TO THE SUKKAH

This idea will give us further insight into the nature of the mitzvah of sukkah, for we see that the sukkah actually partakes of some aspects of the sanctity associated with the Beis Hamikdash. For example, the halachah states that it is forbidden to use the *schach* of a sukkah for mundane purposes. The Gemara derives this from the verse's use of the term "חַג הַסֻּכֹּת,"[21] associating the word חג with the idea of a חגיגה—festive offering:

כְּשֵׁם שֶׁחָל שֵׁם שָׁמַיִם עַל הַחֲגִיגָה, כָּךְ חָל שֵׁם שָׁמַיִם עַל הַסּוּכָּה.

Just as the name of Heaven devolves upon a festive offering, so too, the name of Heaven devolves upon the sukkah.[22]

Correspondingly, we find that the Beis Hamikdash itself is referred to as a sukkah. The verse in *Amos* declares in Hashem's name, referring to the Beis Hamikdash:

---

20   *Shemos* 25:8.
21   *Devarim* 16:13.
22   *Sukkah* 9a.

ביום ההוא אקים את סכת דויד הנפלת:

On that day I will raise up the fallen sukkah of David.[23]

This verse finds expression in the request that we add in to *Birkas Hamazon* over the course of Sukkos:

הרחמן הוא יקים לנו את סוכת דוד הנופלת.

May the Merciful One raise up for us the fallen sukkah of David.

The meaning behind referring to the Beis Hamikdash as a sukkah is that the shade of the sukkah reflects Hashem's direct protection and supervision; hence, the Beis Hamikdash, where the Divine Presence is most felt, represents the ultimate sukkah. On Sukkos, which is dedicated to a celebration of our special connection with Hashem, we offer a prayer that the ultimate sukkah, where that connection is fully realized, will be rebuilt.

What emerges from the above is that the sukkah embodies an amazing combination of the two elements that represented Hashem having His Presence dwell among us in the *midbar*:

- The *Ananei Hakavod* that surrounded us
- The *Mishkan* that stood at the center of our encampment

THE ARBA MINIM—FOUR THAT ARE ONE

This fundamental idea regarding Sukkos will also give us further insight into the second mitzvah of the festival—the *arba minim* (four species). There is a well-known comment of the Midrash that associates the four species with four types of Jew:[24]

- The *esrog* (citron) has taste and fragrance, representing Jews who have both Torah learning and good deeds.
- The *lulav* (palm branch) comes from a date tree that produces fruit but does not have fragrance, representing those who have Torah learning but not good deeds.

---

23   9:11.
24   *Vayikra Rabbah* 30:12.

- The *hadas* (myrtle) has fragrance but no taste, like those Jews who have good deeds but no Torah learning.
- The *aravah* (willow) has neither taste nor fragrance, corresponding to those who have neither Torah learning nor good deeds.

Accordingly, on Sukkos, the Torah commands that we take all these species together, symbolizing the coming together of all Jews. Yet we may ask: Notwithstanding the crucial value of unity among the Jewish People, that is true throughout the year. Why is Jewish unity being highlighted specifically on Sukkos?

However, bearing in mind that Sukkos celebrates the special connection between Hashem and the Jewish People, we must also recognize that this connection is only fully enabled when the people are as one. This idea is expressed by R' Moshe Chaim Luzzatto, who writes that since Hashem is One, He only fully connects with an entity that is likewise "one"; hence, His connection with the Jewish People is dependent on them being together as one.[25] Therefore, the festival that celebrates our Divine connection with Hashem also contains a mitzvah that emphasizes what makes that connection possible—the togetherness of the people as expressed so beautifully by the bringing together of the *arba minim*.

---

25   *Maamar Hachochmah.*

CHAPTER 2

ZMAN SIMCHASEINU–
THE TIME OF OUR JOY

INTRODUCTION: IN THE PRAYERS–AND IN THE VERSES

When each of the festivals is mentioned in the *Amidah* for that day, it is accompanied by a description of that festival. Thus, we refer to Pesach as "זמן חרותנו—the time of our freedom," and to Shavuos as "זמן מתן תורתנו—the time of the giving of the Torah." When it comes to Sukkos, we refer to it as "זמן שמחתנו—the time of our joy." This final description requires our attention, for it seems to be rather non-specific in nature—are not all the festivals times of joy?

What makes the joy of Sukkos distinct from that of all the other festivals?

In truth, as much as the halachah states that there is a mitzvah of *simchah* on all the festivals, when we look at the relevant verses we see that the Torah does not actually mention joy explicitly in connection with Pesach, and does so only once with regard to Shavuos.[1] However, when it comes to Sukkos, there are three mentions of being joyous.[2]

---

1   *Devarim* 16:11.
2   *Vayikra* 23:39, *Devarim* 16:14 and 15.

Thus, we see that the Torah itself seems to be highlighting the element of joy in Sukkos specifically. Still, the question is, Why?

BAALEI HATOSAFOS–STAGES IN THE HARVEST

An answer to this question, from an agricultural standpoint, is offered by the *Tosafos*. We note that the three *Regalim* occur at key points in the agricultural cycle, and are referred to as such in the Torah. Pesach is called "חג האביב—the festival of the ripening,"[3] Shavuos is "חג הקציר—the festival of the reaping,"[4] and Sukkos is "חג האסיף—the festival of the ingathering," when the grain is brought in from the fields.[5] Accordingly, *Tosafos* explain that on Pesach, when the produce has ripened, there is not yet joy as there are numerous stages yet to go before one can harvest it. On Shavuos, when the produce has been reaped, there is already an element of joy. By contrast, Sukkos is the time when all the produce has been gathered in and one thus rejoices over the harvest in full measure.

BETWEEN CLOUDS AND HUTS

Recognizing the three *Regalim* as they relate to the yearly harvest will help us explain something else about Sukkos. In the previous chapter, we mentioned the idea that when the verse commands us to dwell in sukkos, in commemoration of the sukkos in which we dwelled in the *midbar*, the reference is to the *Ananei Hakavod* that surrounded us there. This is the opinion of Rabbi Eliezer, and it is the one adopted by the *Tur* and *Shulchan Aruch*. However, the Gemara states that Rabbi Akiva disputes this view and understands that the reference is to actual huts. Needless to say, of the above two opinions, the second one seems very difficult to understand. It is not so hard to accept the notion that we would have a festival commemorating the Clouds of Glory. They were, after all, a miracle! However, what are we to make of the Torah giving us

---

3   See *Shemos* 23:15 and 34:18 where the Torah refers to Pesach as taking place "למועד חודש האביב—At the time of the month of ripening."
4   *Shemos* 23:16.
5   Ibid.

a festival that commemorates our dwelling in huts? They hardly seem worthy of celebration!

The *Rashbam* explains that the commemoration of huts fulfills a vital function, for Sukkos is the festival of the gathering.[6] It is the time when the harvest that had been in the fields over the summer has been gathered in. At such a time, there is great feeling of accomplishment and satisfaction. This could easily lead a person to forget the One Who is the real source of his success, and he may instead attribute his harvest to his own agricultural acumen and industrial prowess. At this time, the Torah commands us to leave our houses and remember that we began our history as a nation living in huts in the middle of the desert. Hashem took us from there and brought us to the Land of Israel. This reminder of Hashem's kindness to us from the outset serves to give crucial perspective to all our subsequent successes in the land He gave us.[7]

TWO TRACKS OF YOM TOV

Let us take this discussion one stage further. R' Yitzchak Hutner explains that if we survey the various days the Torah has mandated as festivals, we will see that they fall under two categories, or cycles:

- The *Shalosh Regalim*: Pesach, Shavuos, and Sukkos
- The *Yamim Noraim*: Rosh Hashanah and Yom Kippur

What is most fascinating is that the festival of Sukkos is actually the culmination of *both* of those cycles.[8]

With regard to the three *Regalim*, the Torah explicitly mentions Sukkos as the final *Regel* after Pesach and Shavuos.[9] Upon closer inspection, we will see that it also represents the summation of the *Yamim*

---

6   Commentary to *Vayikra* 23:43.
7   We will note that this explanation provides an alternative answer to the *Tur*'s question regarding why the commemoration of our sitting in huts takes place during the month of Tishrei and not in Nissan, since Tishrei is when the harvest is gathered in, and hence, when this appreciative perspective is most needed.
8   *Pachad Yitzchak, Yom Hakippurim* 8.
9   *Devarim* 16:16.

Noraim. This is apparent when we take a deeper look at the mitzvos of the festival.

As we discussed in the previous chapter, the *Vilna Gaon* explains that although we received the clouds immediately upon leaving Egypt, we subsequently lost them as a result of the *Cheit Ha'eigel.*[10] With the atonement we received on Yom Kippur, the clouds returned to stay with us on the fifteenth of Tishrei, signifying the resumption of the special intimate relationship between us and Hashem. This is why we celebrate Sukkos in Tishrei, for we wish to commemorate the *Ananei Hakavod*—not when we originally got them, but when we got them back.

When we consider these words of the *Vilna Gaon,* we will see that the mitzvah of sukkah highlights and celebrates the power of *teshuvah* (repentance), for it was through *teshuvah* that we merited having the clouds returned to us.

A similar idea can be seen in the second mitzvah of Sukkos, the *arba minim.* In discussing this mitzvah, the Midrash explains that when someone has a court case against him, one way to know whether or not he has been successful is to see if he emerges from the court waving his weapons triumphantly. Similarly, we wave our *lulav* as a sign of our confidence that Hashem has accepted our *teshuvah* on Yom Kippur and has atoned for our sins, allowing us to be vindicated in our judgment.[11] This demonstrates that a key element within this mitzvah, too, is that of celebrating our atonement on Yom Kippur.

SUKKOS—A DOUBLE YOM TOV

It thus emerges that through both mitzvos of Sukkos, the theme of celebrating *teshuvah* pervades the festival, making it the concluding festival of the *Yamim Noraim,* as well as of the *Shalosh Regalim.* Moreover, the Gemara tells us that during the special celebrations accompanying the drawing of the water (*Simchas Beis Hashoeivah*) that took place on Sukkos in the Beis Hamikdash, there was a special song sung by those who had

---

10   See *Targum* to *Shir Hashirim* 2:17.

11   *Midrash Tanchuma, Parshas Emor* 18.

done *teshuvah* and returned to Torah and mitzvos.[12] This underscores the idea that a central part of the celebrations on Sukkos is over having succeeded in doing *teshuvah*.

The important idea that emerges is that just like the agricultural aspect of the festival is of yearly relevance to the farmers, so too, the aspect of celebrating *teshuvah* is not merely a commemoration of how our ancestors' *teshuvah* was accepted all those years ago in the desert—it is relevant to each person every year as they emerge from the days of Rosh Hashanah and Yom Kippur.

In light of these two elements within the festival, let us recall the dispute between Rabbi Akiva and Rabbi Eliezer regarding which sukkos we are commemorating. We saw that Rabbi Akiva says we are commemorating actual huts we lived in, while Rabbi Eliezer says we are commemorating the *Ananei Hakavod* that accompanied us. Putting these two discussions together, we will see a very beautiful illustration of the concept of *"eilu va'eilu divrei Elokim chaim*—Both these and these are the words of the living God." The full picture comprises both of these opinions; their dispute hinges on which is considered primary:

- We saw that one aspect of Sukkos is that of *regel*, celebrating the completion of the harvest. In this respect, we commemorate the actual huts we lived in while in the desert, for as the *Rashbam* explained, this will keep us from becoming haughty as we bring in the harvest.
- The second aspect of Sukkos is celebrating the atonement through *teshuvah* on Yom Kippur. To this end, we commemorate the *Ananei Hakavod*, which, as we have seen, came back to us in the month of Tishrei as a result of our atonement for the *Cheit Ha'eigel*.

In fact, upon further reflection, it is possible to say that Sukkos is actually two festivals rolled into one!

---

12   *Sukkah* 53a.

We can now begin to appreciate why even though every festival is a time of joy, we nonetheless refer to Sukkos as the quintessential *zman simchaseinu*, for Sukkos is the culminating festival not only of the three *Regalim*, but also of the *Yamim Noraim*—celebrating not only the harvest, but also the acceptance of our *teshuvah*.

This profound idea is stated explicitly in the Midrash,[13] where it explains that the reason the Torah mentions the concept of joy repeatedly in connection with Sukkos is a product of two things:

- The yearly harvest has finally been gathered in.
- The Jewish People have received atonement on Yom Kippur.

This second element is especially meaningful for each of us every year, and adds a very personal dimension to the national commemoration of Sukkos. We have all been through the special days of Rosh Hashanah and Yom Kippur; we have done *teshuvah* and received *kapparah*. The *Ananei Hakavod* were so called because they demonstrated the special relationship that exists between the people of Israel and the glory of the Divine Presence. Through the purification of the *Yamim Noraim*, each of us has had his own "*Ananei Hakavod*" restored and his connection with the Divine Presence reestablished. There is no greater gift we could ask for, and our appreciation of this gift should accompany us and permeate the days that we call *zman simchaseinu*—the time of our joy.

COMPLETING THE PROCESS

In truth, the relationship between joy and atonement goes beyond the idea of one being a celebration of the other. The term *teshuvah* literally means "returning," for more than anything else, sin serves to distance a person from Hashem, and the *teshuvah* process is about getting back together with Him and restoring the closeness that should exist. In this regard, the process of return that begins with atonement culminates with joy. The Gemara states, "The Divine Presence rests

---

13   *Yalkut Shimoni, Parshas Emor*, sec. 654.

only on one who is in a state of joy."[14] It is only in joy that a person's spiritual faculties are fully active and are receptive to achieving a higher connection with Hashem. Therefore, the joy of Sukkos enables us not only to celebrate the distance that has been closed through atonement, but to enable it to be closed even further, as through it we reclaim our closeness with Hashem.

---

14   *Shabbos* 30b.

CHAPTER 3

SUKKOS AND THE LAND OF ISRAEL

The Torah introduces the mitzvos of Sukkos, i.e., dwelling in the sukkah and taking the *arba minim*, with the words, "באספכם את תבואת הארץ—When you gather in the produce of the harvest."[1] These words clearly indicate that the mitzvos of Sukkos were only to be initiated once the Jewish People entered the land. However, as we will see, not only do these mitzvos *apply* once the people enter the land—they are *about* the people entering the land.

IN THE RISHONIM: THE ABARBANEL AND THE RAMBAM

The *Abarbanel*, in his commentary to *Vayikra*,[2] explains that the *arba minim* express the beauty of the Land of Israel, and that the *aravos* (willows) in particular give thanks to Hashem for bringing us to a place where there are streams and other bodies of water available.[3] This idea

---

1   *Vayikra* 23:39.
2   Ibid., verse 40.
3   See also *Abarbanel*, end of *Parshas Re'eh*, where he echoes this theme, suggesting further that the festival of Sukkos is seven days long corresponding to the seven species of produce over which the Land of Israel is praised. R' Shlomo Fisher (*Drashos Beis Yishai, drush* 1 for Sukkos)

23

is also expressed by the *Rambam* in the *Moreh Nevuchim*,[4] who goes further and states that the two mitzvos of Sukkos—sukkah and *arba minim*—reflect the situation of the Jewish People in the *midbar* and the Land of Israel, respectively. Through the sukkah we recall that we initially dwelled in huts in the *midbar*, and through the *arba minim* we celebrate Hashem bringing us from the *midbar* into the Land of Israel:

> *The [four] species express our joy at having left the wilderness, which could not support any vegetation and where there was no water, to a place of fruit-bearing trees and rivers. In recognition of this, we take of the most choice of the fruits, which has a pleasant aroma, and the most beautiful of the branches and leaves.*

A fascinating and most significant theme thus emerges regarding the festival of Sukkos, namely, that it is a celebration of our entering the Land of Israel. In this regard, it constitutes a fitting culmination to the other two *Regalim*-festivals, Pesach and Shavuos, which celebrate our freedom and receiving the Torah, respectively. This element of Sukkos is perhaps easy to overlook, since the mitzvos of the festival apply in all locations, not just in Israel. What emerges is that although there are many mitzvos in the Torah that apply only in the Land of Israel, the festival that celebrates receiving the land itself is for all Jews, wherever they are.

YEHOSHUA AND EZRA: TWO SPECIAL SUKKOS CELEBRATIONS

This idea will also give us further insight into the verse's description of the first Sukkos celebrated by those returning from the Babylonian exile in the days of Ezra:

ויעשו כל הקהל השבים מן השבי סכות וישבו בסכות כי לא עשו מימי ישוע
בן נון כן בני ישראל עד היום ההוא ותהי שמחה גדולה מאד:

> *The entire congregation that had returned from captivity made sukkos, and they dwelled in sukkos. For the Children of Israel*

---

likewise suggests that this idea is the basis of the time-honored custom of having the seven species as decorations in the sukkah.

4   3:43.

*had not done thusly from the days of Ye[ho]shua bin Nun until
that day, and there was very great joy.*[5]

As we will appreciate, it is highly unlikely that the verse means to
say that the mitzvah of Sukkos itself was not fulfilled between the days
of Yehoshua and that time almost a thousand years later.[6] Indeed, the
verse does not say that they did not make sukkos in the intervening
generations, but that they had not "done thusly." Rather, given that the
celebration of Sukkos is over our entry into the Land of Israel, we will
appreciate that the festival had not been celebrated as it had been in
the days of Yehoshua, when we first entered the land, until the days of
Ezra, when we once again returned, as the verse concludes, "and there
was very great joy."

HOSHANOS AND THE WALLS OF JERICHO

It is very interesting, in light of this idea, to see the imprint of our
entry into the land on our celebration of Sukkos on a yearly basis. One
of the special additional sections of the prayers on Sukkos is *Hoshanos*,
during which we circuit the *bimah* once each day during the first six
days of the festival and seven times on the seventh day. As we will discuss in a later chapter, the *Talmud Yerushalmi* explains that this pattern
is based on the way in which the Jewish People were instructed to act
during their very first battle upon entering the Land of Israel.[7] They circled the walls of Jericho once each day for six days, and on the seventh
day, they encircled the city seven times, whereupon the walls crumbled.
It is most fascinating that the inaugural conquest of the Land of Israel
finds this commemorative expression in the festival that is dedicated to
thanking Hashem for the land.

THE ANANEI HAKAVOD AND THE LAND OF ISRAEL

Now, we should not lose sight of the fact that the verse itself states
that the reason we sit in sukkos is to commemorate the sukkos in which

---

5   *Nechemyah* 8:17.
6   As the Gemara (*Arachin* 32b) expresses it: "Can it be that David came and did not celebrate
     Sukkos, until Ezra came and did so?"
7   *Sukkah* 4:3.

we dwelled in the *midbar*.[8] Seemingly, the idea that Sukkos celebrates our entry into the Land of Israel fits very well with the view that our sukkos commemorate actual huts; for, as the *Rambam* writes, we remember how Hashem took us from those huts to the Land of Israel. However, how does this work with the view—adopted by the *Tur* and *Shulchan Aruch*—that our sukkos commemorate the *Ananei Hakavod*?

In order to answer this question, we need to explore the role and significance of the Land of Israel. Our deep relationship with the land is not just because, as a people, we need a land of our own. If that were the case, then *any* land could fulfill this purpose. Rather, the uniqueness of the land lies in its sanctity and in it being the focus of Hashem's direct and immediate supervision. This idea is expressed by the verse in *Sefer Devarim*:

ארץ אשר ה' אלקיך דרש אתה תמיד עיני ה' אלקיך בה:

A land that Hashem, your God, seeks out; the eyes of Hashem, your God, are always upon it.[9]

The directness of Hashem's supervision of the land reflects the idea that the ultimate closeness to Him is attainable only there. Hence, the Gemara states, "One who dwells outside of Israel is as if he has no God,"[10] meaning, he is missing out on the direct connection that exists there.[11]

With this in mind, we can understand how the idea of Sukkos celebrating our entry into the Land of Israel is a direct progression from the *Ananei Hakavod* that the sukkah commemorates. For as we have seen, those clouds represented Hashem's presence among us during our time in the *midbar*. As such, we proceed to celebrate our entering the land, where that relationship and closeness can achieve their full potency.

---

8   *Vayikra* 23:43.
9   11:12.
10 *Kesubos* 110b.
11 See *Ramban* to *Vayikra* 18:25.

Taking this discussion one stage further, we note that the Torah twice makes a point of linking the idea of Sukkos with the gathering of the harvest:

- In *Parshas Emor*, we find, "באספכם את תבואת הארץ...בסכת תשבו שבעת ימים—When you gather in the produce of the land...you shall dwell in sukkos for seven days."
- In *Parshas Re'eh* it says, "חג הסכת תעשה לך שבעת ימים באספך מגרנך ומיקבך—You shall make for yourself the festival of Sukkos for seven days, when you gather in [the produce] from your threshing floor and your winepress."

Given that dwelling in the sukkah commemorates the *Ananei Hakavod* in the *midbar*, what does that have to do with gathering in the harvest? How are these two ideas related to each other?

A basic manifestation of the Land of Israel as a land where "the eyes of Hashem, your God, are always upon it," is that our experiences in the land will be an expression of Hashem's direct supervision. One of the places where this is most manifest is in the yearly harvest. This is a direct result of the rains that fall in the land, which are in turn judged by Hashem on an ongoing basis in response to the behavior and standards of the people in the land, as we are told numerous times throughout the Torah. Hence, at the time when we gather in the harvest, we celebrate, not only the harvest itself, but the Divine guidance that gave it to us. Therefore, at this time, we dwell in sukkos and recall the *Ananei Hakavod*, for *the very same closeness* between Hashem and us that was expressed by those clouds in the *midbar* is now being expressed by the harvest we have just brought in.[12]

As we noted, the mitzvah of sukkah applies equally outside the Land of Israel as well as in the land. However, once we appreciate that the festival of Sukkos is a celebration of receiving the land, dwelling in the sukkah should awaken within us a yearning and aspiration to

---

12   R' Leib Mintzberg, *Ben Melech*, *Sukkos*, chap. 1.

return to the Land of Israel. How fitting it is, therefore, that the *Yehi Ratzon* prayer recited as part of the *Ushpizin* liturgy concludes with the following words:

ותזכנו לישב ימים רבים על האדמה אדמת קודש, בעבודתך וביראתך.

And grant us the merit to dwell many days upon the land, the Holy Land, in Your service and in Your awe.

May we merit to see the fulfillment of this prayer, speedily in our days!

CHAPTER 4

SUKKOS, JOY, AND PEACE

There are two concepts that are intimately bound up with the festival of Sukkos: joy and peace.

- Sukkos is referred to as "the time of our joy."
- The sukkah is associated with peace, as we say in our prayers, "Spread over us the sukkah of Your peace."

Let us consider the role of these two concepts within the festival.

JOY

Rav Kook explains the progression from the *Yamim Noraim* to Sukkos in the following way. The days of Rosh Hashanah are dedicated to engaging in *teshuvah* and attaining atonement. The process of *teshuvah* requires, by definition, feelings of soul-searching, regret, and self-reproach, as we realize that many of the things we did over the course of the year were not correct. This process is absolutely necessary in order to relinquish our misdeeds and change our improper ways. As such, having successfully done *teshuvah*, a person will naturally be in a somewhat subdued state.

However, while this state was crucial when it was needed for the *teshuvah* process, it cannot accompany and define the person moving forward. At this stage, it is necessary to reinstate joy in our lives, for a person is only fully alive and effective when they are happy. Therefore, the Torah provides us with the festival of Sukkos—the time of our joy—after Yom Kippur, in order to reawaken our feelings of happiness so that they be put to positive use in allowing us to live Torah as it should be lived—with full verve, vigor, and joy.[1]

PEACE

A similar dynamic exists regarding Sukkos and the concept of peace. The Torah states that the reason for the mitzvah of dwelling in the sukkah is "so that your generations may know that I caused the Children of Israel to dwell in sukkos when I took them out of Egypt."[2] The *Hakesav V'Hakabbalah* explains that the term *"hoshavti"* in our verse is not just to be understood as referring to dwelling, but also to being settled,[3] as we find elsewhere "נפשי ישובב—He shall settle my soul."[4] Accordingly, the point of the mitzvah is to recall how Hashem provided conditions in the *midbar* for the Jewish People to be in a settled state.

Why is it important to remember this every year, and what does it have to do with us?

Once again, we go back to the days that precede Sukkos—Rosh Hashanah and Yom Kippur—which are dedicated to the theme of *teshuvah*. It is fair to say that the number one impediment to doing *teshuvah* is complacency. It is an impressively alarming quality of human beings to be able to remain complacent in the face of exhortation or remonstration. This quality is described and discussed by no less than Moshe Rabbeinu who, as he exhorts the people, informs them that there may be some among them who, even upon hearing the dire curses for those who violate the Torah and mitzvos, "will bless himself in his heart saying, peace will be with me, for I will do as my heart sees fit."[5]

As long as a person is complacent, either satisfied that they are doing "just fine," or at peace with the things they are doing that are not

---

1   *Oros Hateshuvah*, chap. 9.
2   *Vayikra* 23:42.
3   Commentary to *Vayikra* ibid.
4   *Tehillim* 23:3.
5   *Devarim* 27:18.

fine at all, they are beyond the reach of *teshuvah*. Any call to mending or improving their ways will fall on deaf ears. Indeed, the very notion of trying to do better will not even register in any meaningful sense.

The work of *teshuvah* thus has as its imperative first step that of making the person uncomfortable regarding their faults and shortcomings. The first key juncture in this process is Rosh Hashanah. The sound of the shofar on Rosh Hashanah is, as the *Rambam* famously explains, an alarm call, "Wake up from your slumber!"[6] For one who falls prey to complacency can effectively sleepwalk peacefully through life for years.

This process continues through the *Aseres Yemei Teshuvah* (Ten Days of Repentance) and reaches its high point on Yom Kippur. The central theme of Yom Kippur—encompassing the fast and all the other restrictions of the day—is that of *inuy*, usually translated as "affliction." Thus, the words with which the Torah presents the fast, "ועיניתם את נפשותיכם,"[7] are commonly translated as "you shall afflict your souls." However, I believe a more practical and accessible translation of the term *inuy* is "agitation." This translation can be demonstrated from the following halachah:

Although it is forbidden on a Torah level to eat or drink even a minute amount on Yom Kippur, there is a certain amount, known as a *shiur*, which has a much greater level of severity. (Often, people for whom it is dangerous to fast will be instructed to eat and drink in increments of less than these amounts at a time.) What are the *shiurim* for eating and drinking? In almost all areas of Torah, the significant amounts of food and drink are a *kezayis* (the volume of an olive) for food, and a *reviis* (approximately three fluid ounces) for liquids. On Yom Kippur, however, the amounts are different. The *shiur* for food is the volume of a dried date, while for liquids it is the amount that fills one's cheek. What is behind these unusual amounts? The Gemara explains that these represent the amounts of food and drink that would "מייתב דעתיה של אדם—settle a person's mind."[8]

---

6   *Hilchos Teshuvah* 3:4.

7   *Vayikra* 23:27.

8   *Yoma* 79b.

Working backward from this definition, we would say that if the fast has been "broken" when one eats or drinks enough to be settled, the definition of *inuy*, and the goal of the fast, is to make one unsettled or agitated. In terms of our discussion, we can well understand why this is so. If the veneer of being settled is not broken, the day can come and go without being accessed and used in any meaningful way. This is the role of the fast, to break free from the state of complacency, so that the work of *teshuvah* on Yom Kippur can happen.

However, as much as being settled is a debilitating impediment when it prevents a person from doing *teshuvah*, it is a crucial asset in the performance of mitzvos, for a person cannot function effectively as a Jew while he is in a state of agitation and anxiety. Therefore, having ousted peace in the form of complacency when doing the wrong thing, it then needs to be reinstated as confidence and security when doing the right thing. To this end, immediately following the days of *teshuvah*, the Torah provides us with a festival dedicated to commemorating the peace of mind Hashem afforded us by surrounding us with the *Ananei Hakavod*. By engaging in and connecting to these special days, we can the reclaim that peace of mind in our own Jewish living as we move forward into the year ahead.

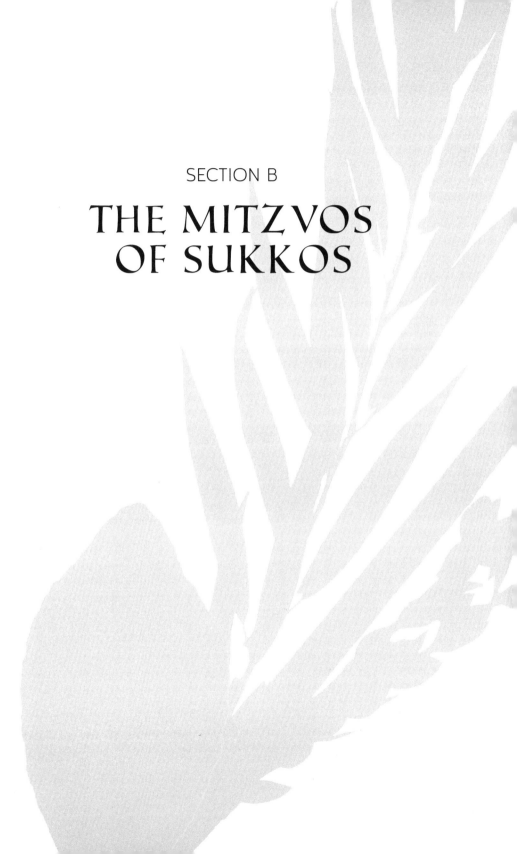

SECTION B

THE MITZVOS
OF SUKKOS

CHAPTER 5

THE SUKKAH

The mitzvah of sukkah has numerous specifications—both in terms of dimensions and of materials—for the walls and for the *schach*. On a surface level, these specifications are purely practical in nature. However, when we contemplate them further, we can see that contained within them are profound messages related to the core themes of the festival. Let us discover and discuss some of these messages.

SUKKAH–AN EMBRACE OF DIVINE DIMENSIONS

The halachah informs us that the minimum dimensions required for a sukkah are "two complete walls and a *tefach* [handbreadth]."[1] These are very specific dimensions; they are, in fact, unique to the mitzvah of sukkah. The *Arizal* explains these unique requirements by referring us to the verse in *Shir Hashirim*: "שמאלו תחת לראשי וימינו תחבקני—His left hand under my head, and his right hand embraces me."[2] The first half of the verse refers to the days of Rosh Hashanah and Yom Kippur, which are days of judgment. The "left hand" represents the attribute of judgment, and thus we refer to those days as ones where "Hashem's left hand supports our head." The second half of the verse refers to Sukkos,

---

1 *Sukkah* 4b.
2 8:3.

which are days of Divine love and mercy, represented by Hashem's "right hand embracing me." Considering the walls of the sukkah in this light, we note that the two complete walls, with a *tefach* for the third wall, represent an arm embracing those in the sukkah. In light of the nature of the days of Sukkos, we see that the sukkah is nothing less than a "Divine embrace." Hashem has invested the walls of the sukkah with a message representing His love for us.

THE SCHACH

The requirements for materials used for *schach* on top of the sukkah are as follows:

- They must grow from the ground.
- They must not be attached to the ground.
- They must not be susceptible to receiving *tumah* (ritual contamination).

The source for these requirements is based on the Gemara's exposition on the Torah's words "חג הסכת תעשה לך שבעת ימים באספך מגרנך ומיקבך"—You shall make the festival of Sukkos for seven days, when you gather in from your threshing floor and from your winery."[3] Although the *pshat* (simple meaning) of the words "באספך מגרנך ומיקבך" refers to the timing of the festival, when the harvest is gathered in, the Gemara expounds them as also referring to the materials that can be used for the *schach* on top of the sukkah, "פסולת גורן ויקב"—that which remains from the threshing floor and the winery."[4] This teaches us that one may use the shells and branches that grow from the ground, and have been detached from it but are not susceptible to receiving *tumah*. This last requirement excludes the fruit itself, which can contract *tumah*.

What is the lesson here? Why are the qualifications of kosher *schach* communicated to us in this way?

The shells and branches of produce are not the primary entity. Rather, their role is to support and contain the fruit. The Torah commands us

---

3   *Devarim* 16:13.
4   *Sukkah* 12a.

to use *these* materials as the roof of our sukkah in order to emphasize that our physical possessions likewise exist only in a supporting and containing capacity for spiritual and moral living, which is the primary "fruit" of life. These items become the roof of our abode during the festival and, indeed, as surely as one can see through the *schach* and perceive something higher beyond it, so too, one should be able to see beyond his physical possessions, recognizing that they are not of ultimate value.[5]

A TEMPORARY DWELLING

In the same vein, numerous commentators write that this idea is the reason behind another one of the basic requirements for the sukkah, namely, that it should be a temporary dwelling.[6] This is to remind us that our dwelling in this world is likewise not of a permanent nature, thereby encouraging us to invest in matters of ultimate value.[7] Now, in suggesting such a reason—or any reason—for the mitzvah of sukkah, we need to be mindful of the fact that the Torah itself has already provided the reason: to remember the *Ananei Hakavod* that accompanied us in the *midbar*. How do these two reasons intersect?

The *Malbim* explains that in order to extend Divine protection to the Jewish People in the *midbar*, Hashem could have chosen any medium with which to surround them.[8] They could have been surrounded by shady trees that miraculously followed them wherever they went, just as Miriam's well did. Yet the medium Hashem chose through which to protect them was that of clouds, which are something that generally resides in the heavens. By surrounding them with a heavenly entity,

---

5   *Drashos Rabbeinu Yosef Nechemiah*, p. 94.

6   What is the source for the idea that the term "sukkah" denotes a temporary dwelling? According to the *sefer Revid Hazahav* (*Bereishis* 33:17), the answer comes from the verse in *Parshas Vayishlach* where sukkos are mentioned for the first time in the Torah (ibid.): "ויעקב נסע סכתה ויבן לו בית ולמקנהו עשה סכת"—Yaakov journeyed to Sukkos and built for himself a house, and for his livestock he made shelters [sukkos]." If we look closely at the verbs used by the verse in describing Yaakov's actions, we see that it says he *built* a house for himself and *made* sukkos. This teaches us that unlike a house, which is "built," on account of it being a permanent structure, a sukkah is simply "made," for it is temporary in nature.

7   See, for example, commentaries of the *Malbim* and *Hakesav V'Hakabbalah* to *Vayikra* 23:43.

8   Commentary to *Vayikra* ibid.

Hashem created a heavenly setting and atmosphere, encouraging the people be constantly mindful of higher goals and to prioritize them accordingly. Dwelling in a temporary abode thereby reflects that message that physical endeavors are secondary to spiritual ones.

Spelling Out the Message

The verses that present the mitzvah of sukkah read as follows:

בסכת תשבו שבעת ימים כל האזרח בישראל ישבו בסכת. למען ידעו דרתיכם כי בסכות הושבתי את בני ישראל בהוציאי אותם מארץ מצרים.

You shall dwell in sukkos for seven days; every native in Israel shall dwell in sukkos. In order that your generations will know that I caused the Children of Israel to dwell in sukkos when I took them from the land of Egypt.[9]

It is noteworthy that the first two times the word "sukkos" is mentioned in these verses, it is written missing a *vav*—"סכת," while the third time it is written in a "fuller" way, with a *vav*—"סכות."

The sukkah is meant to remind us of the *Ananei Hakavod* with which Hashem surrounded us in the *midbar*. How does it do that? Although the walls of the sukkah surround us, they do not in any way resemble clouds! Wherein, then, lies the reminder? Through dwelling in the sukkah—which is a temporary abode—and taking its lessons to heart regarding what is primary and what is secondary in this world, we enable ourselves to connect to the message of the *Ananei Hakavod*; namely, of residing with and being enveloped by the Divine Presence while yet in this world.

Thus, when the verses mention the sukkos we are to build in performance of the mitzvah, they are spelled deficiently, without a *vav*, for they are indeed deficient structures. By contrast, when the verses refer to the sukkos we are meant to meaningfully recall and connect with, they are spelled with a *vav*, for those sukkos represented the ultimate dwelling in Hashem's abode.

---

9   *Vayikra* 23:40–42.

JOY AND VISION

Notably, the de-emphasis of physical living as an essential value occurs during the festival known as *"zman simchaseinu*—the time of our joy." True joy comes from involvement in meaningful pursuits. Attaining a perspective on what is of primary and of secondary value in life allows a person to invest the best of their energies in the former, thereby enabling him to attain true joy.

Indeed, the idea of restoring correct vision is essentially bound up with the concept of the sukkah. Numerous commentators point out that the word *"sukkah"* is related to the term *"socheh,"* which means "to see";[10] for the goal of the sukkah is to enable a person to see things as they should be seen.

In terms of timing, the festival occurs when the harvest is gathered in. It is at this time that a person most needs to know the true place their material prosperity occupies within their system of values, in order to use it in the most beneficial and meaningful way possible.

However, as we have noted, the timing of the festival of Sukkos is also significant in terms of following on directly from Rosh Hashanah and Yom Kippur, and reflects the fact that it is, in many respects, a continuation or progression of the *Yamim Noraim*. This gives us an important insight into the mitzvah of living in a sukkah, for it is there to help us implement the changes we would like to bring about in our lives. Much of the climate that allows for our mistakes is based on mistaken priorities, losing sight of what is important and what isn't. To live our lives in light of what we have learned on and from Rosh Hashanah and Yom Kippur, we need to restore a balanced and healthy perspective on our relationship with the world. In this regard, both Yom Kippur and Sukkos play a role:

- Yom Kippur initiates the process of reclaiming this perspective by temporarily ceasing all significant physical activity and interaction with the physical world. This "time out" allows us to recalibrate our vision of the world and our relationship with it.

---

10   See, for example, Rabbeinu Bachya, *Kad Hakemach*, s.v. *"sukkah."*

- Sukkos continues this process by applying the same method, not to what we *do*, but to what we *own*. Although we need to own things, we need to ensure that they do not take over and become a value in themselves. Our homes and possessions are meant to serve us, but if we don't maintain our sense of perspective, we can easily end up serving them.

The mitzvah of sukkah takes us out of the house and in so doing de-emphasizes it and liberates us from it. The week spent in the sukkah, under the shade of the *schach*, allows us to reflect *through experience* on what we really need and what is really important. It is true that we do not spend our entire lives in the sukkah; at some point we will reenter our homes. However, the goal is that when we do finally come back inside on Shemini Atzeres, it will be with the perspective we gleaned and absorbed over the seven days spent in the sukkah.

SCHACH, WALLS, AND BITACHON

The very first discussion in *Maseches Sukkah* relates to the acceptable height of a kosher sukkah. The opening Mishnah states that if a sukkah is higher than twenty *amos* (cubits), it is invalid.[11] According to one of the explanations given in the Gemara, the reason for this is that one needs to be in the shade of the *schach* in order to fulfill the mitzvah. If the walls are higher than twenty *amos*, one is no longer in the shade of the *schach*; rather, he is now in the shade provided by the walls themselves.[12]

What is the significance of this idea? What is the ultimate difference between sitting in the shade of the *schach* and the shade of the walls?

A most profound explanation of this matter is provided by R' Yaakov Ettlinger.[13] He prefaces by referring us to the well-known discussion in

---

11   *Sukkah* 2a.
12   The Gemara notes that according to this approach, the maximum height of twenty *amos* is stated where the sukkah has the minimum length and breadth of seven *tefachim* (hand-breadths). If the sukkah would be larger than that, it could be higher as well while still allowing the person to be in the shade of the *schach*.
13   *Aruch Laner, Sukkah*, siyum for *Maseches Sukkah*.

the Midrash regarding Yosef's request of the chief butler to remember him to Pharaoh. The Midrash sees this request as a breach in the area of *bitachon* (trust in Hashem) and, moreover, states that Yosef was punished for these words by having to spend two extra years in jail.[14] Needless to say, this Midrash requires some explanation. How are we meant to understand this indictment of Yosef? Notwithstanding Yosef's exalted spiritual level, was he expected to do *nothing*? We know that there is a concept called *hishtadlus* (investing effort) that accompanies one's trust in Hashem. Was not the chief butler—who was about to be reinstated to his position with Pharaoh—a reasonable avenue for such *hishtadlus*?

One of the classic verses relating to the matter of *bitachon*—well-known to us from the end of *Birkas Hamazon*—reads as follows:

ברוך הגבר אשר יבטח בה' והיה ה' מבטחו.

Blessed is the man who trusts in Hashem, and Hashem will be his security.[15]

Seemingly, this verse has said the same thing twice: for if a person trusts in Hashem, surely that means that Hashem is his security! Why does the verse feel the need to spell this out?

Rav Ettlinger explains that, in fact, it is possible for a person to trust in Hashem but at the same time have something else as his security. This occurs when one engages in a certain form of *hishtadlus* with the assumption that if success comes, it will certainly come through this avenue. In this case, even if he trusts that blessing and success will not come unless Hashem bestows His blessing—so that he does indeed trust in Hashem—nevertheless, he has placed his action as his "security" in terms of what will make things work. In truth, full trust in Hashem means that even as one engages responsibly and diligently in actions that could reasonably help his situation, in the end, he trusts in Hashem to grant him blessing and success through *whatever means*

---

14   See *Bereishis Rabbah* 89:2.

15   *Yirmiyahu* 17:7.

He judges appropriate. In this way, not only does the person trust in Hashem regarding the result, but ultimately, Hashem—and not the avenue of *hishtadlus* in which he invested—is also his security in terms of how that result will come about.

With this in mind, let us come back to Yosef's request from the chief butler to remember him to Pharaoh. The verse reads:

כי אם זכרתני אתך כאשר ייטב לך ועשית נא עמדי חסד והזכרתני אל פרעה
והוצאתני מן הבית הזה:

If only you will remember me...and you will please do me a kindness and you will mention me to Pharaoh, then you will get me out of this place.[16]

With these words, Yosef was indicating that *the only way* he would be able to leave his prison cell would be if the chief butler would remember him to Pharaoh. We can be in no doubt that Yosef knew that this endeavor would not succeed without Hashem's blessing, so that he trusted fully in Hashem, nevertheless, he was indicted for having the chief butler—and not Hashem—as his security.

As we have discussed, one of the primary themes of the festival of Sukkos is Hashem's protection and supervision of His people, as embodied by the *Ananei Hakavod* that accompanied them through the *midbar*. The walls of the sukkah represent a person's *hishtadlus*, upon which he places the *schach*, representing Hashem's supervision. There is no question that one needs both in order to have a kosher sukkah. The critical question, however, is, in *whose shade* does one reside? If the walls are too high, then even though the *schach* is ultimately on top of them, nevertheless, the person resides in the shade of the walls, laying essential emphasis on his *hishtadlus*—and hence, the sukkah is invalid. Rather, the *schach* needs to be placed on top of the walls in a way that the person is directly in the shade of the *schach*, reflecting his full reliance on Hashem, not only in terms of *what* will happen, but also *through what* it will happen. That is a kosher sukkah.

---

16   *Bereishis* 40:14.

CHAPTER 6

THE NAMES WITHIN THE WALLS

ARIZAL: THE SUKKAH AND THE TWO NAMES OF HASHEM

There is a well-known statement of the *Arizal* that the word "sukkah" comprises a combination of two names of Hashem:

- *Havayah*—*Yud-Hei-Vav-Hei*
- *Adnus*—*Aleph-Dalet-Nun-Yud*

This is because the numerical value of the *Shem Havayah* is twenty-six, while that of *Adnus* is sixty-five. The two of these together equal ninety-one, which is the numerical value of the word sukkah.[1]

Needless to say, these words are extremely esoteric. Let us try and ponder them and glean from them a message that is accessible and meaningful for us regarding the mitzvah of sukkah.

VILNA GAON: A NAME WITHIN A NAME

Commenting on the above idea, the *Vilna Gaon*[2] notes that not only does the word sukkah *equal* the total of the above two names, it actually *contains* one of the names inside the other. By this he means that the

---

1   *Pri Eitz Chaim, Shaar HaSukkos*, chap. 4.
2   Commentary *Yahel Ohr* to *Zohar, Parshas Pinchas*, cited by R' Dovid Cohen, *Zman Simchaseinu*, chap. 22.

middle two letters of the word סוכה are כו, whose value is twenty-six, representing the *Shem Havayah*, while the outer two letters are סה, whose value is sixty-five, the same value as the *Shem Adnus*.

Here, too, we ask, what is the significance of one name being contained within the other? And what does all this have to do with the sukkah?

The *Vilna Gaon* then draws our attention to the verse in *Chavakuk*, which states:

וי-ה-ה-ו-ה בהיכל קדשו:

And Hashem is in His holy sanctuary.[3]

He explains that the verse is indicating that the *Shem Havayah* itself is "contained in a sanctuary." And what is that sanctuary? The word for sanctuary, היכל, also has the numerical value of sixty-five, representing the *Shem Adnus*. It turns out that the *Shem Adnus* is the sanctuary or chamber that houses the *Shem Havayah*—paralleling the idea that the outer letters סה in sukkah "contain" the letters כו.

These words, too, are very esoteric. What does it mean for one name of Hashem to be a "chamber" in which another name "resides"?

TWO FORMS OF DIVINE INTERACTION

To understand how the *Shem Adnus* is the chamber that contains the *Shem Havayah*, we need to uncover a basic layer of meaning regarding these two names:

- The *Shem Havayah* refers to Hashem as the One behind all existence (הויה). A corollary of this is that this name is associated with Hashem's performance of open miracles, for the One Who gave existence its original nature can override and alter that nature if He so desires.
- The *Shem Adnus* refers to Hashem as Master (אדון) of the world, Who oversees and runs it on an ongoing basis, specifically, within the rules of nature that He set up.[4]

---

3   2:20.
4   R' Yitzchak Chaver, introduction to *Binyan Olam*.

With this in mind we can understand the idea of the *Shem Havayah* being housed within the *Shem Adnus*. This represents the fact that Hashem Who created everything and can change anything at any time (*Havayah*), nevertheless, clothes His interaction within the boundaries of nature that He set up (*Adnus*). The core concept expressed in Hashem's governing of nature is essentially no different than that which is expressed in His performance of miracles; all that has changed is the manner through which He interacts with the world.

As we have seen, this concept is embodied by the mitzvah of sukkah. While we were in the *midbar*, Hashem demonstrated His relationship with us by miraculously surrounding us with *Ananei Hakavod*. Once we move from the *midbar* and transition into natural life, that *very same relationship* continues to exist; it is just that now it is expressed through more natural means, such as peace, prosperity, and a successful harvest. The Torah thus commands us that as we sit in our sukkah, we should remember the *Ananei Hakavod* and the connection they represented, and then reflect upon and celebrate the continuity of that connection in our natural lives.

Thus, we can now understand the significance of the *Shem Havayah* (כו) being contained within the *Shem Adnus* (סה) in the word סוכה. For the sukkah teaches us that the mode of Divine interaction represented by the *Shem Havayah* indeed lies at the core of the interaction as expressed by the *Shem Adnus*. Nature itself is full of miracles.

Indeed, coming back to the verse in *Chavakuk*, which informs us that the *Shem Adnus* is the "chamber" for the *Shem Havayah*, we note that it concludes with the following words:

הס מפניו כל הארץ:

Let all the world be silent before Him.

The silence of the world before Hashem that the verse discusses represents its recognition and ultimate acceptance of His dominion. It is fascinating to consider, in light of the *Vilna Gaon's* idea mentioned above, that the word "הס" (silent) comprises the two letters *hei* and *samech*, the two outer letters in the word "sukkah," which, as we have seen, form the chamber of the *Shem Havayah* and its expression of Hashem's supervision of the natural world.

AVRAHAM'S MESSAGE

The above discussion will give us deeper insight into a statement of the Gemara, that from the day the world was created, no one referred to Hashem by His name until Avraham did so, as recorded in *Bereishis* 15:7.[5] *Tosafos* raise a simple question: Avraham was not the first person in the Torah to use Hashem's name![6] Noach did so hundreds of years beforehand, when he said "ברוך ה' אלקי שם—Blessed is Hashem, God of Shem."[7] *Tosafos* answer that Noach used the *Shem Havayah*, while Avraham was the first one to use the *Shem Adnus*. What does this mean? The *Rashba* explains that many people in Avraham's time believed in Hashem as the Creator; they just felt that He had since abandoned the world to lower forces who were thus deserving of their worship.[8] By introducing the *Shem Adnus*, Avraham was emphasizing that Hashem not only created the world but also continues to supervise and control it. Indeed, the Midrash relates that Avraham spread this message to his guests. When wayfarers would benefit from Avraham's hospitality and would offer their thanks, he would reply that they should instead thank Hashem, Who had provided the food.

Roots

With this in mind, perhaps we can understand a somewhat obscure comment of the Midrash, which states that in reward for Avraham telling the three guests to sit under a tree while he prepared food for them,[9] he merited that his descendants would receive the mitzvah of sukkah. The Midrash is not necessarily implying that the tree itself was a kosher sukkah—it was presumably attached to the ground, which would

---

5   *Berachos* 7b.
6   Ibid., s.v. "*lo*."
7   *Bereishis* 9:26.
8   *Chiddushei Aggados*, *Berachos* loc. cit.
9   See *Bereishis* 18:4.

disqualify its branches for being used as *schach*, in addition to which, his non-Jewish guests were certainly not obligated in the mitzvah of sukkah! Rather, the intent is that in reward for his taking his guests in and imparting to them the message that Hashem provides for their welfare on an ongoing basis, his descendants merited the mitzvah of sukkah, which embodies this message.

YERUSHALAYIM AND SHALEM

There is a most intriguing comment of the Midrash regarding the origins of the name Yerushalayim.[10] Originally, the city was called Shalem, as we find in reference to Malkitzedek the king of Shalem in *Parshas Lech Lecha*.[11] Subsequently, at the time of the *Akeidah*, Avraham called the place Yireh, when he prayed that "ה' יראה—Hashem will see."[12] Hashem did not want either of those names to be neglected, and so He combined them both and called the city "Yerushalayim" (יראה-שלם).

What is the significance of these two names and of their being combined into one?

The commentators explain that originally, the city was called Shalem, which means "perfect," as it was known to be a place that was perfect (שלם) in every way.[13] However, in the eyes of the populace, who did not factor in any notion of ongoing Divine interaction, the perfection of the place was a product of the inherent qualities with which it had been endowed at the time of Creation, and nothing more. To this end, and in keeping with his mission of alerting people to Hashem's continual supervision and control of the world, Avraham added the name Yireh. With this, he came to enlighten people as to *why* this place was so special, namely, that it was the most concentrated setting of the Divine Presence that resided there. The name Yireh means "will see," and with this name, Avraham was emphasizing that Hashem will continually see and supervise mankind, and nowhere more so than in the city of

---

10   *Bereishis Rabbah* 56:10.
11   *Bereishis* 14:18.
12   Ibid., 22:14.
13   See *Ramban* to *Bereishis* 14:18.

Shalem. As a result of all this, Hashem combined the two names into one, so the name would reflect both the special nature of the city and the basis of that uniqueness.[14]

This gives us added insight into a verse in Tanach that refers to the city as Shalem even after it had been called Yerushalayim, a verse that appears specifically in connection with Sukkos. In chapter 76 of *Tehillim*, it says:

ויהי בשלם סוכו ומעונתו בציון:

Then His [Hashem's] sukkah was in Shalem, and His dwelling in Zion.[15]

The sukkah mentioned in the verse refers to the Beis Hamikdash. As we have discussed, the reason the Beis Hamikdash is called a sukkah is because, like a sukkah, it reflects Hashem's shade, i.e., direct supervision. Thus, with the Beis Hamikdash itself actively communicating Avraham's message—for which reason he added the name Yireh—the city itself can once again be referred to by its original name, Shalem.

TOWARD A COMPLETE SUKKAH

It is worthwhile mentioning in conclusion the classic comment of R' Shlomo Hakohen of Vilna,[16] who notes that throughout the Chumash and Tanach, the word "sukkah" is always written without the letter *vav*: סֻכָּה. The only exception is in the abovementioned verse in *Tehillim*, "ויהי בשלם סוכו ומעונתו בציון." According to the Midrash, this verse refers to future times when Hashem's "sukkah," i.e., the Beis Hamikdash, will be in Shalem, i.e., Jerusalem.[17] However, R' Shlomo Hakohen points out that there is also an allusion here. Hashem's supervision of the world is not currently recognized by all. The war against such recognition was originally led by Amalek, who sought to eradicate any notion of Divine interaction and the personal responsibility and accountability that

---

14 *Vilna Gaon,* commentary to *Shir Hashirim* 7:1.
15 *Tehillim* 76:3.
16 *Cheshek Shlomo,* end of *Maseches Sukkah.*
17 *Midrash Tehillim,* chap. 76.

come with it. Accordingly, the Midrash states that Hashem's name will not be complete until Amalek has been destroyed.[18] Therefore, since, as we have seen, the word sukkah likewise contains two names of Hashem, it too is not written in complete form in the Tanach. However, in future times, when the final redemption has arrived and Amalek and all that he stands for has been destroyed, then Hashem's name will be complete and the word sukkah, too, will be able to be written in full. Thus, the verse says, "Hashem's sukkah will be complete [shalem], when His dwelling will be in Zion."

May we merit to see this, speedily in our days!

---

18   Cited in *Rashi* to *Shemos* 17:16.

CHAPTER 7

USHPIZIN

BACKGROUND

One of the time-honored customs relating to the mitzvah of dwelling in the sukkah is that of *Ushpizin*, inviting seven of our illustrious ancestors as guests in our sukkah. This custom is based on the practice of Rav Hamnuna Sava, as cited in the *Zohar*.[1] Before entering his sukkah, he would stand at the entrance and say, "Let us invite the guests and prepare the table...be seated exalted guests, be seated, be seated guests of faithfulness, be seated."

WHY ONLY ON SUKKOS?

It is worthwhile considering that while there are other festive meals throughout the year, we do not invite these special guests to those meals, e.g., to our Shabbos table or to our Seder table. This practice is restricted to our meals in the sukkah. A beautiful explanation of why this is so is found in the writings of the *Sefas Emes*,[2] based on a teaching of his grandfather, the *Chiddushei HaRim* of Gur. In the opening chapter of *Hallel*, we praise Hashem as One Who "מאשפות ירים אביון, להושיבי עם נדיבים, עם נדיבי עמו—raises up the destitute from the trash heaps, to seat them

---

1   *Parshas Emor* 103b.
2   *Sukkos* 5652.

with nobles, with the nobles of His people." We have just gone through the days of Rosh Hashanah and Yom Kippur, where we ourselves were destitute of merits. Through these exalted days, Hashem has raised us up from the trash heaps and granted us atonement. Accordingly, the next step is that He allows us to sit with the nobles of our people, our illustrious ancestors, as we invite them as guests into our sukkah.

Beautiful!

INVITATION AND EMULATION

Perhaps we may suggest an additional reason why the *Ushpizin* are invited specifically on Sukkos. The seven *Ushpizin* are as follows:

1. Avraham
2. Yitzchak
3. Yaakov
4. Yosef
5. Moshe
6. Aharon
7. David

The above list has the *Ushpizin* in chronological order, and this reflects the mainstream Ashkenazic custom. However, these seven personalities also each embody one of the attributes that make up the lower seven *Sefiros* (Divine emanations), which represent the way through which Hashem interacts with the world, and the custom of the *Arizal* is to order them accordingly:

1. Avraham—*Chessed* (Kindness)
2. Yitzchak—*Gevurah* (Strength)
3. Yaakov—*Tiferes* (Splendor)
4. Moshe—*Netzach* (Eternality)
5. Aharon—*Hod* (Glory)
6. Yosef—*Yesod* (Foundation)
7. David—*Malchus* (Kingship)

Based on this correlation, numerous sources write that part of inviting the *Ushpizin* on Sukkos includes ourselves trying to emulate the attribute personified by the guest of that particular day.[3] Indeed, perhaps we can now understand on a deeper level why we invite these guests specifically on Sukkos. We have seen how Sukkos is dedicated to celebrating the special connection between Hashem and the Jewish People. Although on a fundamental level this connection is constant, nonetheless, it can be developed and strengthened by our own conduct. The more we emulate Hashem's ways, the closer to Him we get. Hence, the seven days of Sukkos are devoted to taking our connection and raising it to ever higher levels, through emulating the *middos* embodied by the *Ushpizin*. Indeed, perhaps it is for this reason that the *Zohar* proceeds to stipulate that if a person has not seated the needy as guests in his sukkah—or has not otherwise made provisions for their Yom Tov needs—the *Ushpizin* do not join him there either.[4] If an integral part of *Ushpizin* is internalizing and emulating the attributes of the *Ushpizin*, with whom we are seated after having ourselves been destitute, it must begin by us looking out for the destitute and needy among our own, raising them up and seating them with honor and respect.

---

3   See, for example, *Michtav MeEliyahu* 2:110 for a presentation of this daily *avodah*.
4   Ibid.

CHAPTER 8

THE FOUR SPECIES

INTRODUCTION: A SYMPHONY OF FOUR

One of the central mitzvos of Sukkos is the *arba minim*, the four species, which are taken on every weekday of the festival.[1] As we know, the mitzvah is only fulfilled by taking all the four species, and in this respect, they are all partners in the one mitzvah. At the same time, each of the species has distinct qualities that are worthwhile reflecting upon in terms of their contribution to the mitzvah and to the overall theme of Sukkos.

THE ESROG

The Gemara notes that the *esrog* tree has an unusual characteristic in that its fruit tastes like its bark. Hence, when the Torah describes the *esrog* as *"pri eitz hadar"*[2] (fruit of a citron tree), the two juxtaposed words *"pri"* and *"eitz"* ("fruit" and "tree"), are expounded to mean "the fruit is like the tree."[3]

---

1   On a Torah level, the mitzvah of *arba minim* applies on all seven days only in the Beis Hamikdash. In all other locations, the mitzvah applies only to the first day. After the destruction of the Beis Hamikdash, the Sages instituted that the mitzvah be performed on all seven days everywhere as a *zecher laMikdash*, a remembrance of how it was—and will be—performed in the Beis Hamikdash.
2   *Vayikra* 23:40.
3   *Sukkah* 35a.

We should realize that this characteristic goes beyond being simply a curious anomaly, for *Tosafos* inform us that it is in recognition of this quality of the *esrog* that it was chosen to be one of the *arba minim*.[4] The background to this is that initially, all fruits were meant to have this property whereby the fruit would taste like the tree. Thus, Hashem's command on the third day of Creation was that the earth produce *"eitz pri*,"[5] once again denoting the parity between the tree and the fruit. However, the earth did not fulfill this equation, bringing forth instead, as the verse either way describes, *"Eitz oseh pri*—Trees that produce fruit," but the tree itself did not have the taste of the fruit.[6] It thus emerges that the only fruit that remained faithful to the original command was the *esrog*, and thus it merited to be included in the mitzvah of the *arba minim*.

Expansion in Torah and in Creation

There is a further point here, for in truth, the *pshat* meaning of the words *"eitz pri"* would really seem to be "trees that produce fruit." The interpretation that "the tree is like the fruit" seems to be the product of Midrashic exposition, which equates the two words. It turns out that the fault of the trees was that they neglected to make this exposition, following instead the *pshat* meaning of the words!

Interestingly, this was not the only opportunity for exposition of Hashem's words on that day. The Midrash teaches further that although Hashem only mentioned the idea of *"lemineihu*—within its particular species"[7] regarding trees, nevertheless, the shrubs and bushes also came forth in their distinct species. The Midrash proceeds to explain that this was based on a *kal vachomer* (a fortiori argument), for they reasoned as follows: If Hashem commanded the trees, which do not naturally get mingled with each other, to come forth with their distinct species, then we bushes, who do have a natural tendency to get mixed

---

4   *Tosafos Hashalem* to *Bereishis* 1:11.
5   *Bereishis* 1:11.
6   Cited in *Rashi* to *Bereishis* ibid.
7   *Bereishis* ibid.

up with each other, how much more so should we see to it that we come forth with each species distinct.[8]

This is a truly amazing situation, for it turns out that the first *kal vachomer* in history was actually the product of a grassroots movement!

And yet, at the same time, the basic premise of these Midrashim is understandably somewhat baffling. What are we to make of all these learned expositions that were reasoned, or meant to be reasoned, by the trees and bushes?

Perhaps the explanation of the matter is as follows: The *Zohar* explains that the very first entity to be created by Hashem was the Torah, which then formed the energy from which creation emerged in increasingly lower and more physical worlds.[9] Creation has many parts to it, which in turn reflect different aspects of Torah. Thus, for example, the illumination of Torah is represented by light (day one), and its sustaining quality is represented by water (day two). Yet there is also an element of Torah that increases and develops through the expositions and reasonings of the Oral Law, to deal with ever new situations and questions as they arise. Which element of Creation parallels this part of Torah? The answer is: the third day, which brought forth entities that can grow and expand. As such, the enterprise of expositions naturally accrued to plant life. Moreover, at the moment of Creation, which was, in a sense the transitional or interface moment of conversion of Torah energy into created matter, the Torah element was yet present and active, allowing for such expositions to be made.

This quality of the *esrog*, in addition to being praiseworthy for itself, is very closely connected with the festival of Sukkos, which celebrates our special and intimate connection with Hashem. The failure of the trees to produce fruit that tastes like the tree was not simply the result of "not noticing" the basis to expound Hashem's words. Rather, it was an *active refusal* to do so. The *Chizkuni* explains that the earth reasoned that if trees would taste the same as their fruit, people might not wait

---

8   *Chullin* 60a, cited by *Rashi, Bereishis* loc. cit., verse 12.
9   *Zohar, Parshas Terumah* 161a (see *Nefesh Hachayim* 4:10–11).

for the fruit and instead eat the trees, leading to their depletion.[10] Although the earth does not have free will in the moral sense, nevertheless, as a created independent entity, the earth's spiritual faculties sought to preserve that independent existence. This led it to part ways with the full meaning of Hashem's instructions and, thereby, to loosen its connection with Hashem Himself. By the *esrog* staying true to the full meaning of Hashem's will, it preserved the original connection and hence features so prominently in the *arba minim* on Sukkos, which celebrate that connection.

In our own national experience, this idea found its highest expression in our declaration at Sinai of "*naaseh venishma*—we will do and we will hear."[11] By placing "we will do" before "we will hear," we were indicating our preparedness to accept Hashem's Torah even before knowing what is in it; for by definition, whatever Hashem wants for us, we accept to do. What is most interesting is that this concept, too, is associated with the *esrog*. Commenting on a verse in *Shir Hashirim*, "Like a *tapuach* among the trees of the forest, so too, is My beloved [Israel]," the Gemara states that the Jewish People are compared to a *tapuach*: just as a *tapuach* produces fruit before its flowers, so too, the Jewish People said "*naaseh*" before "*nishma*."[12] Although we commonly translate *tapuach* as "apple," *Tosafos* explain that the reference is, in fact, to an *esrog*.[13] Indeed, the two properties of the *esrog* (fruit tasting like the tree and fruit before flowers) are both expressions of the same idea, namely, the intimate connection with Hashem as expressed in the faithful fulfillment of His will. In this regard, there is much indeed to learn from the *esrog* as we seek to strengthen and develop our own connection with Hashem and His Torah.[14]

---

10   Ibid.

11   *Shemos* 24:7.

12   88a.

13   *Shabbos* ibid., s.v. "*piryo*." The reason the *esrog* is described as producing fruit before its flowers is because the *esrog* fruit stays on the tree from one year to the next, so that it precedes the flowers of the following year.

14   On a more specific level, we noted in the opening chapter that Sukkos commemorates the *Ananei Hakavod* specifically as they returned after we received atonement for the *Cheit Ha'eigel*. That sin itself was primarily based on our compulsion to chart our own course in

THE LULAV

When it comes to the *lulav*, the part that requires the closest inspection is the middle leaf, known as the *teyomes*. This leaf is, in fact, a double leaf, and the halachah stipulates that both half-leaves need to be completely attached to each other.[15] The "togetherness of two" expressed by the *teyomes* is reflective of the special and close connection between the Jewish People and Hashem. In *Shir Hashirim*, which is a depiction of the love between Hashem and His people, He refers to them as "תמתי," which means "My perfect one."[16] The Midrash expounds this term to mean "תאומתי—My twin," reflecting the affinity between us and Hashem.[17] As we have seen, this close connection is the focal point of the celebration of Sukkos and, as such, is fitting to be literally the high point of the *arba minim*. At the same time, the *lulav* itself needs to be straight and upright, indicating that the level of closeness is at its optimum when we ourselves are upright and emulating Hashem's elevated ways.

THE HADAS

The term the Torah uses for *hadasim* is, "עֲנַף עֵץ עָבוֹת."[18] How does this phrase denote *hadasim*? The word "עָבוֹת" refers to a braided rope. Accordingly, *Rashi* explains:

שענפיו קלועים כעבותות וחבלים, וזהו הדס העשוי כמין קליעה.

---

our relationship with Hashem, having approached Aharon not with a question as to what to do in Moshe's absence—but with an instruction to make the calf. In this regard, it was a step down from our pronouncement of "*naaseh venishma*" at Sinai, so that our atonement involved returning to that level, as represented by the *esrog*. This gives us added insight into an idea mentioned in certain classic sources, namely, that the mitzvah of *arba minim* comes to rectify the sin of Adam eating from the *Eitz Hadaas* (Tree of Knowledge). That sin, too, was based on Adam feeling that although he had been commanded not to eat from the tree, his relationship with Hashem would be better served if he ignored that command and partook of the tree, so that his service of Hashem in the post–*Eitz Hadaas* state would be on a higher level than before. In this respect, the *Cheit Ha'eigel* was a rehash of sorts of the sin of the *Eitz Hadaas*, with Sukkos representing a recovery from both of them.

15 See *Sukkah* 32a and *Shulchan Aruch*, *Orach Chaim* 645:3.
16 5:2.
17 *Shir Hashirim Rabbah* ibid.
18 *Vayikra* 23:40.

Whose branches are as braided like cords and ropes, and this is
the hadas [whose leaves are] formed in a braided arrangement.

As we discussed in the opening chapter, Sukkos celebrates the enduring and unbreakable bond between Hashem and the Jewish People. This level of permanence was achieved by Yaakov, the third Patriarch, who is referred to in the verse as "the rope of His [Hashem's] inheritance."[19] Through *Rashi's* words, we see that the braided rope that represents the bond completed by Yaakov is represented by the rope-like plaited leaves of the *hadas*. Indeed, according to the Midrash, the *arba minim* correspond to the three patriarchs and Yosef, respectively.[20] This means that the third of the species, the *hadasim*, corresponds to Yaakov, the third of the patriarchs. Based on the above discussion, we can understand the connection between the two.

Moreover, this may give us deeper insight into the comment of the Gemara that *tzaddikim* (righteous people) are called *hadasim*,[21] for *tzaddikim* maximize the connection between the Jewish People and Hashem that is represented by the braided "rope" of the *hadas*. Moreover, although the Gemara states generally that *tzaddikim* are called *hadasim*, there are two particular instances where this finds expression in the verse itself:

- Esther, who is also called Hadassah[22]
- Chananyah, Mishael, and Azaryah, who refused to bow down to the statue of Nebuchadnezzar during the Babylonian exile, are referred to as *hadasim*[23]

It is these two instances where the *tzaddikim* remained faithful to their higher connection despite immense pressure to abandon it that fully exemplify the strength of the braided rope embodied by the *hadas*.

---

19   *Devarim* 32:9.
20   *Vayikra Rabbah* 30:10.
21   See *Megillah* 13a and *Sanhedrin* 93a.
22   See *Esther* 2:7.
23   See *Zecharyah* 1:8.

From the World of Remez: The Threefold Strand

The idea of the strength of a threefold rope is expressed by the verse in *Koheles*:

והחוט המשלש לא במהרה ינתק:

A threefold cord is not easily severed.[24]

As we have seen, the *hadas* represents a rope that is made up of three strands, thereby ensuring its strength and durability. The *gematria* (numerical value) of the word חוט is twenty-three. When multiplied by three—representing the three strands that can be braided together to become a rope—the result is sixty-nine, which is the numerical value of the word הדס!

THE ARAVAH

The fourth of the species is the *aravah*—the willow branch. As mentioned in the opening chapter, the Midrash associates the *arba minim*, some of which have either taste or smell, both or neither, with four types of Jews in terms of their possession of Torah learning and good deeds. The *aravah*, which has neither taste nor smell, corresponds to those Jews who have neither Torah nor good deeds. Nevertheless, the Torah commands us to take them all together, saying, "Let these come and atone for these."

The above statement is worth reflecting on, for the Midrash does not specify which of the species atone for which. Who are "these" and "these"? Presumably, the reference is to those who are in possession of Torah and good deeds atoning for those who have neither. As such, the *aravah* is purely a beneficiary of being brought together with the other three species. However, the general way in which this idea is phrased lends itself to the possibility that each of the species is a source of atonement for the others. How can this be understood? How can the *aravah*, who is bereft of Torah and good deeds, atone for the species that have those qualities?

---

24   4:12.

The underlying value of feeling a connection and fostering togetherness with Jews who have neither Torah nor good deeds is that at the end of the day, they are Jews. On a surface level, this means that they cannot be abandoned, despite their lack of merit. On a deeper level, it reflects a recognition of the fact that all Jews contain an innate goodness, a spark waiting to be fanned.

Even Jews who possess Torah and good deeds need atonement, for no one is perfect, and every person has areas in which they are remiss or could do better. The basis of receiving atonement in matters where we are substandard is the very same core of purity that we perceive in *aravah*-type people, for our misdeeds do not represent our essential identity or values. In other words, by embracing every Jew as a Jew, simply because he is my brother and is in essence good and holy, we enable ourselves to receive the blessed atonement we all need from the Almighty, notwithstanding our faults, simply because we are His children.

CHAPTER 9

HIDUR MITZVAH–
RECLAIMING GLORY

An idea that features very prominently in the mitzvah of *arba minim* is that of *hidur mitzvah*—beautifying a mitzvah. Whereas in principle this is something that applies to all mitzvos, when it comes to the *arba minim*, it takes on an entirely new dimension. In general, if a mitzvah is lacking in *hidur*, the mitzvah itself is still kosher. However, if one of the *arba minim* on Sukkos is sufficiently lacking in *hidur*, it is completely disqualified. According to *Tosafos*, this is based on the fact that the Torah itself refers to the *esrog* as a *pri eitz hadar*,[1] indicating that *hidur* is an intrinsic characteristic of the *esrog*, and by extension the other species as well.[2]

How are we to understand the crucial role *hidur mitzvah* plays within the *arba minim*?

WHAT MAKES US LOOK GOOD?

The central theme of *hidur* is not to "merely" perform mitzvos, but to reclaim them from the sidelines, where they may have been pushed by other less important things. The things we invest in making beautiful are

---

1   *Vayikra* 23:40.
2   *Sukkah* 29b, s.v. *"lulav,"* based on loc. cit. 31a.

the things that are important to us. This is the (re)orientation of Sukkos, directing our sense of *hidur* and beautification toward mitzvah acts.

Indeed, looked at this way, we can see that the sukkah and the *arba minim* work together as a team, for the sukkah as a temporary dwelling de-emphasizes physical priorities that may have taken over, while the *arba minim* restore mitzvos to the center of our focus and attention where they belong.

There is another layer here. The idea of *hidur mitzvah* with regard to mitzvos generally is derived from the words "זה א-לי ואנוהו—This is my God and I will glorify Him,"[3] which the Gemara explains as communicating the message, "התנאה לפניו במצוות—Beautify the mitzvos before Him."[4]

However, if we look carefully at these words, we will notice that the word התנאה, which is reflexive, does not mean to beautify *something else*, but rather to beautify *oneself*! This means that the verse is saying, "Beautify yourself before Him with mitzvos." This seems rather strange. Since when is beautifying ourselves a value, and what does that have to do with *hidur mitzvah*?

Here we are being taught a profound lesson: everyone has something he takes pride in. Although pride is generally considered an extremely negative character trait, this is only when it is self-serving and egotistical. However, taking pride in something that is greater than oneself can actually be very positive. Anyone who is proud to be Jewish is not exercising bad *middos*, he is expressing something very beautiful and profoundly important. We lose our way when the things we take pride in shift from matters of ultimate importance to those of lesser importance.

Heaven and Earth

The verse in the book of *Eichah* reads, "השליך משמים ארץ תפארת ישראל."[5] The basic meaning of these words is that they are lamenting the fallen glory of Israel, which has been cast down from the heavens to the ground.

---

3   *Shemos* 15:2.
4   *Shabbos* 133b.
5   2:1.

However, there is another underlying meaning. Everyone has his *tiferes*—his sense of glory, the things he takes pride in, the things he boasts about. The problem begins when the *tiferes* of Israel falls from taking pride in heavenly things (שמים) and focuses instead on earthly or temporal things (ארץ).

As we use these days to take stock of our lives and how we have been leading them, an underlying question is, "Where is my *tiferes*? What do I take pride in, and why?"

Much of what we need to do *teshuvah* for by the time Rosh Hashanah comes around can be traced back to this imbalanced perspective that has diverted our *tiferes* from "heaven" to "earth." Hence, a central part of our rehabilitation involves restoring it to its rightful place.

This is the goal of *hidur mitzvah*. When we invest in and beautify a mitzvah, we are saying, "The things in life that make me look beautiful are mitzvos like this one!" In truth, that is the greatest honor we can give to a mitzvah.

And so, as we take our *arba minim* during these seven days, we are reminding ourselves of the things that should make us look good. Those are the things that really count, and they are what deserve our pride, our attention, and our energy. If we can take this lesson and use it to draw up our map of life, the beauty of *hidur mitzvah* will be reflected in everything we do in the year ahead.

PRI EITZ HADAR–BEAUTY FROM THE HEART

It is worthwhile concluding our discussion of the idea of *hidur mitzvah* on Sukkos by returning to look again at the verse where this idea is taught. Although the concept of *hidur mitzvah* applies to all the four species, it is mentioned explicitly only with regard to the *esrog* ("*pri eitz hadar*"), while all the other species are extrapolated from there. There is a very poignant lesson here regarding the entire concept of beauty. The Midrash describes how the each of the *arba minim* represents a significant part of the body:[6]

---

6   *Vayikra Rabbah* 30:14.

- The *esrog* represents the heart.
- The *lulav* represents the spine.
- The *hadasim* represent the eyes.
- The *aravos* represent the lips.

As we know, it is very easy for beauty to become a purely external display, with all emphasis on appearance and none on inner content. To this end, the verse links the concept of *hidur* specifically with the *esrog*, representing the heart, as if to say, the way you carry yourself (*lulav*), look (*hadas*), and speak (*aravah*) in Jewish living should all be a product and expression of how much your heart (*esrog*) cherishes the Torah's mitzvos and values. For true *hidur* comes from the heart.[7]

---

7   R' Moshe Avigdor Amiel, *Drashos El Ami*, vol. 2, *drashah* 1.

CHAPTER 10

TAKING THE FOUR SPECIES

INTRODUCTION: THREE BOUND TOGETHER–
AND ONE JOINED TOGETHER

In preparation for the mitzvah of taking the *arba minim*, three of the species—the *lulav*, *hadasim* and *aravos*—are bound together before the festival. On Sukkos itself, the *"lulav* bundle" comprising those three species is taken in the right hand, the *esrog* is taken in the left hand, and then all four of the species are brought together.

The relationship of the *esrog* with the other three species is thus somewhat complex:

- On the one hand, unlike the other species, it is not bound together with them before the mitzvah is performed.
- On the other hand, it must be brought together with them in order to perform the mitzvah.

What are we meant to make of this?

An insight into the significance of joining together the *esrog* with the other species emerges from an episode that is recounted by the medieval commentator R' Menachem Recannati,[1] as recorded in the *Beis Yosef*:[2]

---

1   *Parshas Emor.*
2   *Orach Chaim* 651.

One needs to join the esrog together with the other species, that it should not be separated [from the group]. This secret was revealed to me in a dream on the first night of the festival of Sukkos, when a certain pious individual from Ashkenaz was staying with me. In the dream, I saw that he was writing the Shem Havayah,[3] and he was distancing the final letter hei from the first three letters. I said to him, "What is this you have done?" and he replied, "This is the custom in our locale." I rebuked him, and wrote the name in its complete [unified] form. I was dumbfounded by this vision and did not understand what it meant. The following morning, at the time of taking the lulav, I saw that he was shaking the lulav and its [attached] species without the esrog and I [then] understood the meaning of my dream. And indeed, the Sages alluded to this secret when they said that...all of the species allude to Hashem, may He be blessed.

We see from the Recannati that the *arba minim* on Sukkos correspond to the four letters of Hashem's Divine name, with the *esrog* corresponding to the final letter *hei*. The importance of joining the *esrog* to together with the other species is that it joins together the final *hei* with the other three letters of the name.

Needless to say, this explanation itself requires understanding. How are these two concepts connected? Moreover, the original question persists: If the *arba minim* are four "letters" in the same "name," why are they not all "written," i.e., attached together, from the beginning?

FOUR LETTERS–FOUR SPHERES

Although the topic of the Divine name known as *Shem Havayah* is extremely esoteric and has infinite levels of meaning, let us at least try and understand it on a basic level that is accessible to us. The commentators explain that the four letters that make up the name correspond to the four levels of existence between Hashem and our world. The first three levels—known as *Atzilus*, *Beriah*, and *Yetzirah* (Closeness,

---

3   The Divine name written *Yud-Hei-Vav-Hei*, known as the Tetragrammaton.

Creation, and Formation)—are essentially spiritual in nature, albeit with each one progressively being a more defined and concretized expression of spirituality. The fourth level is the world of *Asiyah* (Action), which is the physical world in which we live.

Although Hashem's Divine influence naturally flows through the higher three levels, it needs to be connected to the fourth level, the physical world, in order to flow into there as well. Accordingly, the first three species are bound together, reflecting the natural alignment of the first three worlds. The *esrog*, representing the fourth level (the final *hei*), is not bound together with the other three from the outset. Rather, it is our job to join it to them, allowing for Hashem's light to enter our physical world.

This idea is corroborated by a comment of the *Vilna Gaon* regarding our topic:

> The reason the lulav, hadas, and aravah are bound together and not the esrog is because it has been given to man to join together with them, as it says, "השמים שמים לה' והארץ נתן לבני אדם—*The heavens are the heavens for Hashem, and the earth, He gave to man.*"[4]

We see that the first three species and the *esrog* represent the domains of heaven and earth, respectively, with man being tasked with the mission of joining the two together.

RIGHT AND LEFT

This will also give us deeper insight into the specification that the *lulav* and its attached species be taken with the right hand, and the *esrog* with the left, for these two hands also represent the two domains of heaven and earth. Thus, the prophet Yeshayahu declares in Hashem's name:

אף ידי יסדה ארץ וימיני טפחה שמים:

> Even My [left] hand has laid the foundation of the earth, and My right hand has measured out the heavens.[5]

---

4   Commentary *Yahel Ohr* to *Shemos*, cited by R' Dovid Cohen, *Zman Simchaseinu*, chap. 41.
5   *Yeshayahu* 48:13.

By taking the *lulav* bundle in the right hand (representing the domain of heaven) and joining it together with the *esrog* in the left hand (representing the domain of the earth) one allows for a joining of those two domains and the flow of Divine influence from heaven to earth.

All this gives an entirely new level of appreciation of the spiritual qualities and possibilities that exist within the *arba minim*—and of what we are enabling to happen when we bring the *esrog* together with the other three species, even before waving them.

THE MITZVAH IS THE MESSAGE

The idea of joining the higher and lower realms together, which finds concrete expression in the mitzvah of the *arba minim*, is relevant to all of physical living. For it represents elevating physical life heavenward by instilling within it the values and deeds contained in the Torah that we received from heaven. Indeed, based on the verse in *Yeshayahu* cited above, the Gemara says that while "Hashem acts with only one hand, the righteous act with two."[6] This means that while Hashem created the two domains of heaven and earth separately, using a different hand for the each of them, He then left it for the righteous to use both hands together, joining the two domains through their elevated deeds.

THE SUKKAH AND THE FOUR SPECIES

Indeed, in light of this idea, we can see how the two mitzvos of Sukkos—dwelling in the sukkah and taking the *arba minim*—are ultimately connected, and are two expressions of the same concept. As we have seen, the mitzvah of sukkah commemorates the Divine supervision and energy as originally manifested in the miraculous form of the *Ananei Hakavod*, and which continues to flow into the natural world as experienced by the year's harvest. By the same token, the bringing together of the *esrog* with the other three species on Sukkos reflects the way that this flow can be brought downward through the actions of the Jewish People, attaching and aligning the physical world with the spiritual realm by imbuing it with heavenly values and deeds.

---

6   *Kesubos* 5a.

CHAPTER 11

NAANUIM–WAVING THE LULAV

Part of the mitzvah of the *arba minim* involves waving them in all four directions, as well as up and down. Although the basic mitzvah is fulfilled merely by picking the species up, nonetheless, waving them is referred to by the *Rambam* as "*mitzvah kehilchasah*—the full and correct way to do the mitzvah."[1] Indeed, the mitzvah is commonly referred to as "shaking the *lulav*." There are varying customs regarding the order and manner of the *naanuim*. Beyond these practical questions, however, it is certainly worthwhile to try and understand what we are looking to achieve and express by waving the *lulav*.

WINDS, DEWS, AND DIRECTIONS

The Gemara provides two explanations for the waving of the *arba minim* up, down, and in all directions, as follows:

> Said Rabbi Yochanan, "One waves [them] in all directions, toward the One to Whom all directions belong. One waves them upward and downward toward the One to Whom the heavens and earth belong."

---

1   *Mishnah Torah, Lulav* 7:9.

In the West [the Land of Israel] they would say thus, "One waves them in all directions to prevent harmful winds; and one waves them up and down in order to prevent harmful dews."[2]

Regarding the first explanation, although it is, of course, always of value to recognize Hashem as the One to Whom all directions belong, this idea takes on additional significance within the context of Sukkos; indeed, this will provide us with another illustration of how the sukkah and the *arba minim* work together. We have seen how some of the commentators explain that the mitzvah of dwelling in a sukkah comes specifically at the time of the harvest, when a person may feel that he is the master of his own success and that all credit for the harvest goes to him. To this end, the Torah commands us to remember how we initially dwelled in huts in the *midbar*, and how Hashem subsequently took us from there and brought us to the Land of Israel.[3] However, it is still possible for a person to recognize Hashem as the One Who *brought us into* the land, but nevertheless, to ascribe all his success *once he has entered* the land to his own prowess and industriousness. Therefore, when we take the *arba minim*, we wave them up, down, and in all four directions, expressing our recognition of Hashem's ongoing control of all affairs, including the recently completed yearly harvest.

The second explanation for the waving in all directions, namely, to prevent harmful winds and dews, is explained by the Gemara as illustrating the idea that "performing the enhancing aspects of a mitzvah (*sheyarei mitzvah*) has the power to protect a person from calamity."[4] Here, too, we express our hope that in the merit of the *naanuim*, which is the enhancing aspect of the mitzvah of *arba minim*, we will likewise be protected from harm. In this regard, the *Aruch Hashulchan* explains that the concepts of "harmful winds" and "harmful dews" refer to all mishaps and adverse circumstances, which come from all different directions and which are instigated by the Satan—inciting us down below

---

2   *Sukkah* 37b.
3   See chapter 2, citing *Rashbam*.
4   *Sukkah* loc. cit.

and then accusing us on high.[5] Indeed, in this light, it is possible to see how the two explanations of the Gemara (recognizing the One to Whom all directions belong and preventing harmful winds and dews) ultimately go hand in hand. Through our performing the *naanuim* by waving the species in all directions in order to express our recognition of Hashem's control over all directions of the world, we then hope to prevent any mishap from befalling us from any of those directions.

Indeed, the form that each of the individual *naanuim* movements takes is first to move the *arba minim* outward from the heart and then to draw them back inward toward it. For we seek first to express *from* within our hearts the ideas and sentiments contained in the *naanuim*, and then we seek to absorb and embed them *within* our hearts on a deeper level still.

WAVING DURING HODU LAHASHEM AND ANA HASHEM

This idea will explain what would otherwise seem to be a puzzling practice. In addition to when we initially make the blessing over the *arba minim*, we also wave the *arba minim* at specific points during *Hallel*:

- When we say "הודו לה' כי טוב—Thank Hashem, for He is good"
- When we say "אנא ה' הושיעה נא—Please, Hashem, save now"

Of these two, the verse of *Hodu LaHashem* seems an appropriate place for waving as a high point within the *Hallel*. But why do we also wave when saying, of all things "Please, Hashem, save now"?

One of the Rishonim, the *Orchos Chaim*, explains that in this second verse, the relationship between the saying the words and waving the *arba minim* is actually reversed:

- When we wave the *arba minim* while saying, "Thank Hashem for He is good," we do so as an accompanying emphasizing gesture *expressing* the sentiment within those words.
- When we wave while saying, "Please, Hashem, save now," we are asking that *in the merit of* additional enhancing measures

---

5   *Orach Chaim* 651:23.

such as the waving that we are performing now, Hashem should save us from all calamity.

THE SONG OF THE TREES

A further element within the waving of the *arba minim* comes from considering from a different angle the points in the service when this is performed. As we have mentioned, in addition to waving the *lulav* after reciting the *berachah* over it, it is also waved at certain points during *Hallel*: whenever we say הודו לה' כי טוב, and when we say אנא ה' הושיעה נא. Based on a Midrash, *Tosafos* explain the background to waving the *lulav* at these points.[6] The verse says:

אז ירננו עצי היער:

Then the trees of the forest will sing.

The Midrash explains that waving of the *lulav* represents the singing of the trees of the forest. The next verse says, "הודו לה' כי טוב כי לעולם חסדו," and thus we wave the *lulav* whenever we say that verse in *Hallel*. Moreover, the verse after that begins "ואמרו הושיענו אלקי ישענו—And say: 'Save us, O God of our salvation,'" and therefore we also wave when we say "אנא ה' הושיעה נא—Please, Hashem, save now."

This Midrash is telling us something quite remarkable. The waving of the *lulav* itself—aside from the words said—is actually a form of praise. It is a "*Hallel* through action." In fact, this explains to us why we even wave the *lulav* during *Hallel* at all. Although waving the *lulav* is a mitzvah, we do not normally start doing mitzvos when we are already in the middle of doing a different mitzvah. Every mitzvah should have its own time and space! Yet we wave the *lulav* during *Hallel* because it is actually part of *Hallel*. Indeed, a stunning expression of this idea can be found in the *Yerushalmi*,[7] which explains the reason for the disqualification of a dry *lulav*[8] by citing the verse from Hallel itself, "לא המתים יהללו י-ה—The dead will not praise Hashem!"[9]

---

6   *Sukkah* 37b, s.v. "*behodu*."
7   *Sukkah* 3:1.
8   Mishnah, *Sukkah* ibid.
9   *Tehillim* 115:17.

Moreover, it is for this reason that the widespread custom is to make the berachah on the *arba minim* just before *Hallel*, and not at the beginning of the day. This is in order to juxtapose the berachah over the mitzvah to the waving of the *lulav* during *Hallel*, which constitutes the complete fulfillment of the mitzvah.

Still, the question remains: What exactly are we praising Hashem about through waving the *lulav*? Moreover, Sukkos is not the only festival when we say *Hallel*, yet it is the only festival that we give expression to "the song of the trees." Why is this *Hallel* different from all other *Hallels*?

THE GIFT OF NEW LIFE

The answer to this question is found in another comment of the Midrash regarding the mitzvah of *lulav*.[10] It discusses the verse that says, "ועם נברא יהלל י-ה‏—The nation that has been created will praise Hashem."[11] When is this referring to? Have we not already been created?

> אלו הדורות שהן נטוין למיתה, שעתיד הקב"ה לבראותו בריאה חדשה. ומה עלינו לעשות, ליקח לולב ואתרוג ולקלס להקב"ה. לפיכך משה מזהיר את ישראל ואומר להם ולקחתם לכם ביום הראשון.
>
> *These are the generations that are inclined toward death, which Hashem will create anew. And what is incumbent upon us to do? To take a lulav and an esrog and to praise Hashem. Thus Moshe tells the people of Israel, "And you shall take for yourselves on the first day [of the festival] the citron [esrog], the palm branch [lulav], etc."[12]*

The Midrash is informing us that the praise of the *lulav* on Sukkos is over our successfully having made it through the days of judgment. Here again, we see Sukkos acting not only in the capacity of the third *Regel* together with Pesach and Shavuos, but also as the culmination and celebration of the days of Rosh Hashanah and Yom Kippur.

---

10   *Yalkut Shimoni, Vayikra* 651.
11   *Tehillim* 102:19.
12   *Vayikra* 23:40.

This explanation as to the nature of the *lulav*'s praise is actually to be found in the verse cited earlier by *Tosafos*. We have quoted the first half that reads "אז ירננו עצי היער—Then the trees of the forest will sing." The second half of the verse says "מלפני ה' כי בא לשפוט את הארץ—From before Hashem who has come to judge the world." The verse is telling us that the background to the song of the trees is Hashem's judgment of the world that took place on Rosh Hashanah and Yom Kippur.

A WAVE OF GRATITUDE

When considered carefully, the above words of the Midrash are truly astounding, and they should give us a completely new appreciation for what has happened during the first days of Tishrei:

- Should we ask: What are we praising Hashem for by waving the *lulav*? The answer is nothing less than: for having created us anew!
- And should we proceed to ask: Why would we need to be created anew? The answer is: because we were "inclined toward death."

Strict justice demands that if we have been involved in sin, we have forfeited our existence: "הנפש החוטאת היא תמות—The soul that sins, it should die."[13] When Hashem grants us atonement on Yom Kippur in response to our *teshuvah*, He is renewing our lease on existence; He is "creating us anew"!

Interestingly, this idea is reflected in the halachah. The Gemara tells us that if one sees a friend whom he has not seen for thirty days, he recites the berachah of "שהחיינו" to express his joy. The Gemara further states that if he has not seen that friend for over twelve months, he recites the berachah "ברוך מחיה המתים—Blessed is the One Who revives the dead."[14]

This seems to be a rather dramatic way of saying hello!

Why should we express our feelings in this way?

---

13   *Yechezkel* 18:4.
14   *Berachos* 58b.

The *Maharsha* explains that if one has not seen his friend for over twelve months, it means that in the interim that friend has gone through the days of judgment beginning with Rosh Hashanah.[15] The fact that the friend is still alive means that he received new life on Yom Kippur, and it is thus entirely appropriate to recite the blessing "Blessed is the One Who revives the dead."[16]

This, then, is our situation as we celebrate our favorable judgment over the days of Sukkos; we have been the beneficiaries of nothing less than a form of *techiyas hameisim* (revival of the dead). It should certainly serve to place the waving of the *lulav* in an entirely new light. Indeed, perhaps we praise Hashem for our new existence through the medium of action because our feelings about this kindness cannot be communicated through words alone. In this regard, the *naanuim* do not just express everything we would like to say—they express more than we could ever say.

---

15   Ibid., quoted in *Mishnah Berurah* 255:4.

16   The *Shelah Hakadosh* (*Rosh Hashanah, Torah Ohr* 16) quotes the *Tolaas Yaakov* who explains in this vein why we insert the sentence, "מי כמוך אב הרחמים—Who is like You, merciful Father," in the second blessing of the *Shemoneh Esreh* that deals with *techiyas hameisim*. This is to emphasize that Hashem's mercy on His creatures even if they have sinned is a form of *techiyas hameisim*.

CHAPTER 12

HALLEL

INTRODUCTION: HALLEL AND SUKKOS

On each day of Sukkos, we recite the full *Hallel*. In this respect, Sukkos differs from Pesach, for although we recite *Hallel* on every day of Pesach as well, full *Hallel* is recited only on the first day (or days) of Yom Tov, while on the remaining days, half *Hallel* is recited. The Gemara explains the reason for this distinction:[1]

- On Sukkos, the number of *korbanos* varies each day. This gives each day a distinct status and significance within the festival and hence, each day receives a full *Hallel*.

- On Pesach, the *korbanos* are uniform throughout the festival, so the distinction of "new *korbanos*" exists only within the first day. Therefore, full *Hallel* is recited only on that day.

In truth, it is possible to perceive particular meaning within the *Hallel* that is recited during Sukkos. As we have discussed, the festival of Sukkos is dedicated to celebrating the special connection and relationship between Hashem and the Jewish People. When we look at the contents of *Hallel*, we see that they are not just words praising Hashem

---

1   *Arachin* 10b.

in abstract. Rather, an underlying theme of *Hallel* is that of praising Hashem as "our God," highlighting all that He has done for us from the time He took us to be His people and throughout our history, both in good times and bad. In this regard, when we say *Hallel*, alongside praising Hashem, we are also exulting in our relationship with Him, which is the very theme of Sukkos itself.

In this regard, it is most worthwhile to ponder the words of *Hallel* through the medium of the commentators over the generations, thereby gaining further insight into the flow of *Hallel* and some of its central themes.

FROM THE HALLEL

הללו את שם ה'...יהי שם ה' מבורך.

Praise the name of Hashem...May Hashem's name be blessed.

The chapter begins by calling on all to praise Hashem's name, and then proceeds to say that His name shall be blessed. This means that not only should He be "praised" as the Almighty Creator, but He should also be "blessed," meaning, recognized as the source of all blessing on an ongoing basis. Indeed, there may be those among the nations who can relate to the idea of praising Hashem, but not to seeing Him as the source of ongoing blessing, for they claim, "Hashem is raised above all nations, His glory is over the heavens!" They claim it is not befitting for God to be involved with mundane earthly matters, for it is only in the heavens that His glory finds a fitting abode.

To this we respond, "Who is like Hashem our God who dwells on high," and yet "lowers Himself to look upon the heaven and earth?" Here, we are stating that although Hashem Himself dwells infinitely high, still He looks upon the earth.

In truth, even the heavens are infinitely lower than He is, so that even to look at the heavens constitutes a "lowering" of His Presence. As surely as He lowers Himself to consider the heavens, so too, He considers the earth and is involved with it, bestowing blessing on an ongoing basis. The full extent of this involvement is that even those who are in the dust and the trash heaps, He raises up, and brings them joy, and this is His praise![2]

בצאת ישראל ממצרים בית יעקב מעם לועז.

When Israel went out from Egypt, the house of Yaakov from a people of a foreign language.

The redemption from Egypt was comprised of two parts:

- The Jewish People, who had been enslaved in Egypt, were delivered from their servitude.
- The unique character of Israel was able to finally express itself, free of its alien Egyptian surroundings.

Corresponding to the aspect of character, the verse refers to "Israel leaving Egypt," for the name Israel represents the higher qualities of the Jewish People. The verse mentions this aspect first in order to emphasize the primacy of spiritual elevation that came with the Exodus. Corresponding to the physical deliverance from subjugation the verse describes "the house of Yaakov leaving a people of a foreign language."[3]

היתה יהודה לקדשו ישראל ממשלותיו.

Yehudah became His sanctifier, Israel His dominions.

The singling out of the tribe of Yehudah for special mention here is a reference to the fact that it was the prince of Yehudah, Nachshon ben Aminadav, who displayed complete faith in Hashem by jumping into the Red Sea even before it split.[4]

---

2   *Malbim* commentary to *Tehillim* 113.
3   *Maharal, Gevuros Hashem,* chap. 62.
4   *Rashi* to *Tehillim* 114:2. The word "Yehudah" is a masculine noun and is treated as such throughout the Torah and Prophets. In our verse, however, it uses the feminine form "היתה" instead of the masculine "היה." This is an allusion to the fact that Nachshon's act of self-sacrifice was a product of the legacy of his grandmother Tamar, who was prepared to let herself be burned so as not to publicly shame Yehudah (see *Bereishis* 38:24–25, with commentary of *Rashi* [commentary *Maaseh Nissim* to the Haggadah]).

מַה לְּךָ הַיָּם כִּי תָנוּס...מִלִּפְנֵי אָדוֹן חוּלִי אָרֶץ.

What is with you, O sea, that you flee...tremble, O earth, from before Hashem, from before the God of Yaakov.

Why do we ask the sea why it flees? The answer would seem to be obvious: if it doesn't do so, the Jewish People will drown!

The sea's answer is even more perplexing: "Tremble, O earth, from before Hashem, etc." It doesn't seem to have answered the question at all. The sea was asked *why* it fled, not *before whom!*

The description of the sea as "fleeing" represents the fact that it parted abruptly on account of the fierce wind that forced it to move. Strictly speaking, the passage of the Jewish People through the sea could have come about through somewhat more natural means, e.g., through a gradual drying up of that portion of the seabed. That being the case, the question is specifically not "why did you part?"—for which the answer is obviously in order to let the Jewish People pass through—but rather "why did you *flee*?" Why did you part in a way that was so unnatural? How did that contribute to the deliverance of the Jewish People?

The sea answers: It is true that if the only goal of my splitting was to allow the Jewish People safe passage through, I would not have had to split in this blatantly unnatural way. However, that wasn't the only goal.

Indeed, the reason why the miracle of the sea splitting took the form of it "fleeing" was twofold:

- "Tremble, O earth, before Hashem." By parting in this miraculous way, awareness was increased of Hashem as Creator—and Ruler—of the world;
- "Before the God of Yaakov." Hashem wanted to demonstrate the special connection that exists between Him and His people, and that He supervises and guides the events that they experience.[5]

---

5   *Netziv,* commentary *Imrei Shefer* to the Haggadah. See there for a similar explanation of the other two events mentioned in this chapter, "The Jordan [river] turned back," i.e., the river stopped and piled up at the point where the Jewish People crossed over into Israel. A more natural way would have been for it to slow down to a trickle at their point of passage.

לא לנו ה' לא לנו כי לשמך תן כבוד על חסדך על אמיתך.

Not for us, Hashem, not for us, but for Your name give glory,
for the sake of Your kindness and Your truth.

Although we may be lacking in merits that would entitle us to ask for Hashem to protect and deliver us in times of trouble,[6] we nonetheless petition Him to do so for one of three basic reasons:

- "לשמך תן כבוד—For Your name give glory." Since Hashem has attached His name to us, and we are known as His people, our state of degradation constitutes a degradation of the Divine name. We ask Hashem to redeem us, so that through our elevated status people will come to recognize Him in this world.
- "על חסדך—For the sake of Your kindness." Hashem is the epitome of kindness, and His kindness sustains the world constantly. We appeal to Him that His Divine kindness should extend toward delivering us from our exile.
- "ועל אמתך—And for Your truth." Hashem has promised to ultimately deliver us from exile. Having promised us this, the fulfillment of this promise constitutes an expression of His truth.[7]

ברוכים אתם לה' עושה שמים וארץ.

Blessed are you for Hashem, the Maker of heaven and earth.

We should note that the verse does not say "ברוכים אתם מה'—Blessed are you *from* Hashem," but rather "Blessed are you *for* Hashem." The

---

"The mountains skipped like rams." According to the *Netziv*, this refers to the mountains closing in on each other and crushing the Emorites as they lay in ambush for the Jewish People passing through the valley, and then parting again (see *Berachos* 54b). A more natural way would have been an avalanche, or even an earthquake, where the mountains would not subsequently revert to their original locations.

6   The reason why the phrase "לא לנו" is repeated is so it shouldn't sound as if we are *entitled* to ask based on our own merits but are simply *choosing* to pray for redemption for higher reasons. Rather, it is in recognition of the fact that we lack the merit to ask to be redeemed for our own sake, and hence we are asking that Hashem redeem us if only for the sake of His name, kindness, and truth (*Maharal, Gevuros Hashem*, chap. 64).

7   R' Azariah Fego, *Binah L'Ittim, drush* 14.

point of the verse is not to identify Hashem as the source of these blessings but rather to indicate their meaning and purpose. All the blessings Hashem bestows upon the various groups mentioned in the opening verses of this chapter find their ultimate meaning when used for Hashem's purpose as Maker of heaven and earth.

The next verse continues, "השמים שמים לה'—The heavens are the heavens of Hashem." It does not state simply, "השמים לה'—The heavens belong to Hashem." Why mention the heavens twice? The intent is that the fact that the heavens fulfill their purpose *as* the heavens is solely in Hashem's domain, and solely His concern. In contrast to this, "והארץ נתן לבני אדם—He has given the earth to man." Hashem has appointed man as His representative and coworker who is to see to it that the earth fulfills its purpose for which Hashem has created it. It is toward the realization of this goal that the verse states: May all your God-given blessings be used "לה'—*for* Hashem."[8]

אהבתי כי ישמע ה' את קולי...כי הטה אזנו לי.

I loved that Hashem hears my voice...for He has inclined His ear to me.

The straightforward meaning of Hashem "hearing my voice" in this context refers to Him fulfilling the request that was the subject of the prayer. If that is so, we need to consider the meaning of the phrase that follows: "For He inclined His ear to me." This idea is already subsumed within the first phrase, for had He not inclined His ear to me, He would not have fulfilled my request. In fact, the order of the phrases seems to be backward, starting with the ends (fulfilling my request) and only then proceeding to the means (listening to my prayer)!

We see from here that a deeper understanding of the goal of prayer is not merely to have Hashem fulfill one's requests, but rather, through prayer, to establish a connection with Him. It is this connection that is the soul-prize of prayer. In this sense, the fulfilling of the request is not

---

8   R' Samson Raphael Hirsch, commentary to *Tehillim*.

purely its own goal, but also serves a higher purpose of confirming to the person that Hashem was listening to his prayer:

- A simplistic expression would state: "I am happy Hashem inclined His ear to me, for by so doing He heard my voice," i.e., fulfilled my request.
- Our verse expresses the deeper reason for joy: "I am happy that Hashem heard my voice" and fulfilled my request, for that demonstrates to me that "He inclined His ear to me."[9]

מה אשיב לה' כל תגמולוהי עלי.

With what can I repay Hashem for all His kindness to me?

There is, of course, no actual way to repay Hashem for all the kindness He constantly bestows on us. The least we can do however, is to "raise a cup of salvation and call out in Hashem's name," namely, to publicly acknowledge and express our appreciation for all He does for us.

In the times of the Beis Hamikdash, the quintessential expression of gratitude toward Hashem took the form of the *todah* (thanksgiving) offering, which comprised two parts: The offering was brought in the courtyard of the Beis Hamikdash, and then consumed in Jerusalem as part of a thanksgiving feast, during which the person would recount the kindness that was the reason for him bringing the offering.

Corresponding to these two aspects of the *todah* event (the offering and the feast), the verse at the end of this paragraph states, "I will sacrifice a thanksgiving offering to You, and I will call out in the name of Hashem."

The final two verses each contain two phrases. These two phrases do not relate to each other, but rather they follow the format of the two aspects of the *todah* that have been mentioned, and proceed to qualify them respectively, as follows:

---

9   *Pachad Yitzchak, Pesach*, sec. 14.

- "I will fulfill my vows to Hashem" corresponds to the first aspect of the offering of the *todah*.
- "In the presence of all His people" refers to the second aspect of recounting of the miracle at the feast that follows.
- "In the courtyards of the Temple of Hashem" is the setting for the bringing of the offering.
- "In the midst of Jerusalem" is where the thanksgiving feast would take place.[10]

אני עבדך בן אמתך פתחת למוסרי.

I am Your servant, the son of Your maidservant, and You have broken open my bonds.

What does King David mean to say here? He begins by describing himself as a servant of Hashem and proceeds to add "the son of Your maidservant," which emphasizes his complete state of servitude. He then concludes by saying "and You have broken open my bonds," which seems to be a complete negation of everything he said before!

The truth, however, is that every person is a servant, whether to forces inside of him—his impulses and desires, or to forces outside of him—the pressures of societal norms and his peers.

Many people feel "free" in the sense that they do not subscribe to a higher code of living. Practically, this means that they remain shackled by the bonds of all those other forces (internal and external), lacking the wherewithal to release themselves.

King David says, having given my full allegiance to the highest calling, namely, Divine service and Torah living, Hashem has thus released my bonds. Now I have the sense of purpose and fortitude of spirit to resist those other forces when their influence will be detrimental to my spiritual and moral well-being.[11]

---

10   *Netziv, Harchev Davar* to *Vayikra* 7:13.
11   R' Yitzchak Arama, *Akeidas Yitzchak*, sec. 98.

הללו את ה' כל גוים...כי גבר עלינו חסדו.

Praise Hashem, all nations...for His kindness has over-whelmed us.

What do we mean by exhorting the nations of the world to praise Hashem for having overwhelmed *us* with His kindness? This doesn't exactly sound like something that would be expected to elicit much praise from them![12]

First, we need to consider the words "גבר עלינו חסדו," which literally mean that "His kindness overpowered us." What does this refer to? The Talmud tells us that when we stood at the foot of Har Sinai, Hashem suspended the mountain over our heads and said, "If you receive the Torah, well and good, and if not—you will be buried here."[13] The reason for this ultimatum was that the very existence of the world is contingent upon the Jewish People receiving the Torah.[14] It is regarding this episode that we say Hashem "overpowered us with His kindness." Moreover, the result of that act was "Hashem is true to the world [לעולם]," i.e., He faithfully maintains its existence. Thus, all nations owe their existence to this "overpowering kindness" through which we received the Torah, and we exhort them to praise Hashem for it.[15]

A further explanation of these verses is based on the verse in *Bereishis* 15:16. Hashem promises the Land of Israel to Avraham's descendants but stipulates that their entry into the land will not take place straight away, but rather, "The fourth generation shall return here, for the sin of the Emorite is not complete as of yet." In other words, the Jewish People would not be the recipients of Hashem's kindness of entering the land until the indigenous population deserved to be evicted. The Emorite would not be treated unfairly simply because Hashem wished to bestow kindness upon the Jewish People. This is what we are saying when we exhort the nations of the world to praise Hashem: "כי גבר עלינו חסדו," for

---

12   This question, discussed by many commentators, is originally raised in *Pesachim* 118b; see commentaries of *Rashi* and *Rashbam* there for explanations of the Gemara's answer.

13   *Shabbos* 88a.

14   See *Avodah Zarah* 3a, quoted in *Rashi, Bereishis* 1:31.

15   R' Yaakov Ettlinger, commentary *Minchas Ani* to the Haggadah.

even when He is showering us with kindness, nevertheless, "ואמת ה' לעולם," He deals truthfully with the rest of the world, and does not allow the blessing of the Jewish People to be a cause of loss for them.[16]

Our question as to why the nations of the world should be called upon to praise Hashem for the kindness He has shown to the Jewish People was once posed to R' Yitzchak of Volozhin by a certain Russian official. R' Yitzchak responded, "The reason why we tell the nations of the world to praise Hashem for His kindness to us is because, in many respects, they are more qualified to do so than we are. We can only praise Hashem for delivering us from plots and decrees about which we are aware. However, there are countless plots that are foiled and frustrated long before they reach fruition, and about those plots we will never know. The only ones who do know about them are the nations themselves who plotted against us. Thus, we call upon them, being more qualified than us, to praise Hashem for His ongoing kindness toward us."

הודו לה' כי טוב...יאמר נא ישראל...יאמרו נא בית אהרן...יאמרו נא יראי ה'...

Give thanks to Hashem for He is good...Let Israel say...Let the House of Aharon say...Let those who fear Hashem say...

What is the meaning behind dividing the Jewish People into four different groups, if the end result is them all saying the same thing?

The *Chovos Halevavos* states a fundamental principle about expressing gratitude toward Hashem: the more one is a beneficiary of kindness from Hashem, the more one needs to express his appreciation for that kindness.[17] Expressing appreciation is not a generic "one-size-fits-all" exercise, but rather must come from a specific awareness of the particular kindnesses one has received.

The first verse, which says, "Give thanks to Hashem," is not yet addressing the Jewish People. Rather, it is addressing the nations of the

---

16   *Minchas Ani* ibid.
17   *Shaar Avodas HaElokim*, chap. 6.

world referred to above ("Praise Hashem, all nations, etc."). Every living person is a recipient of Hashem's kindness and is obligated to express their appreciation of that kindness.

The second verse, "Let Israel say," goes on to address the Jewish People specifically. Hashem has bestowed upon us kindness of a different order altogether in bringing us close to Him and making us His people; our expression of appreciation for His kindness needs similarly to be on a higher level.

The third verse addresses "the house of Aharon." The Kohanim have been elevated to a higher level and been given certain privileges beyond those of the Jewish People generally, and therefore they need to express their thanks on a higher level as well.

The fourth verse addresses "those who fear Hashem." According to *Rashi*, this term refers to converts. This group has received a still higher level of benevolence in guiding them on their journey toward Judaism, and their expression of praise is thus in a category all on its own.[18]

מן המצר קראתי י-ה ענני במרחב י-ה.

Out of the narrow straits I called to God; God answered me by [granting me] spaciousness.

Hashem's name (י-ה) is mentioned twice in this verse, once in connection with being called from the straits, and again with reference to answering. There are many people who, in times of trouble, look every which way except "up" in order to pinpoint the source of the problem. It does not occur to them that Hashem may be sending them a message—to better their ways or to avoid an unadvisable situation—or that He is the One Who can help them extricate themselves from their predicament.

To this end the verse asserts, "Out of the narrow straits I called to God." Part of one's response to a difficult situation should always be to call out to Hashem for help.

---

18   R' Avrohom Gurwitz, *V'Anafeha Arzei El.*

That said, there are many people who will indeed call out to Hashem in times of trouble, certain that only He can help them. Yet when He sends them the wherewithal to emerge from danger to safety, they somehow forget to identify Him as the source of their salvation after the fact. To this end, the verse states that not only do I call out to Hashem from the straits, but I also recognize Him afterward as the One Who answered me.[19]

עזי וזמרת י-ה ויהי לי לישועה.

God is my strength and my song, and He has always been my salvation.

This verse may be familiar to us, as it features in the song sung by Moshe and Bnei Yisrael at the Red Sea.[20] Our chapter deals with the various dangers and difficulties that the Jewish People encounter throughout history, but Hashem delivers them and does not allow them to be annihilated. In using words that were originally uttered after the splitting of the Red Sea, the verse is not merely utilizing a lofty and eloquent praise found elsewhere in the Scripture. It is actually indicating that the miracle of Jewish survival is of equal magnitude to that of the splitting of the Red Sea![21]

These words resonate clearly with the sentiment expressed by R' Yaakov Emden in the introduction to his commentary on the siddur:

> When one ponders our unique station in this world, we are the flock who is exiled and dispersed. After all that has happened to us with various persecutions over thousands of years; there is no nation as pursued as us…Yet they were not able to overcome us and destroy us. All those ancient and mighty nations, their memory has vanished; while we who cleave to Hashem are alive here, today, together with our Torah…By the life of

---

19   R' Elchonon Wasserman, quoted in the Baranovitch Haggadah.
20   *Shemos* 15:2.
21   R' Samson Raphael Hirsch, commentary to *Tehillim*.

my head I declare, when I reflect on these wonders, they exceed, in my estimation, all the miracles and wonders that Hashem performed for our forefathers in Egypt, in the desert and in the Land of Israel. And the longer the exile continues, the more the miracle becomes manifest in ever greater measure.

CHAPTER 13

HOSHANOS

One of the special features of the service on Sukkos is the *Hoshanos*, where the congregation circles the *bimah* with the *arba minim* in hand, reciting special prayers for salvation.[1] This commemorates the practice in the Beis Hamikdash, as recorded in the Mishnah,[2] whereby the Kohanim would circle the *Mizbeiach* on each day of Sukkos. In our times, the *bimah* takes the place of the *Mizbeiach*, since it is the place where we read about the *korbanos* that are offered on the festival.

THE SHECHINAH IN EXILE

One of the themes that permeates the *Hoshanos* prayers is that of "*Shechinta b'galusa*—The Divine Presence in exile." On a basic level, this represents the idea that Hashem's Presence in the world is intimately tied up together with the experiences of the Jewish People, for it is through their success as a people that He is known to the world. If so, then when the Jewish People are in exile, so too is the Divine Presence, for Hashem's kingship cannot be expressed and is therefore not recognized by the nations. Correspondingly, in this regard, when Hashem

---

1   The two main customs regarding the timing of the *Hoshanos* are either straight after *Hallel* or after *Mussaf*.

2   *Sukkah* 45a.

89

will deliver us from our exile, he will also, so to speak, be delivered with us. Thus, we open the *Hoshana* service by saying, "הושענא למענך אלקינו—Save us, now, for Your sake, our God," and so on.

This idea receives even more explicit expression in the concluding "*Ani Vaho*" section of the *Hoshana* prayers, where we note that the word "*Vayosha*—He [Hashem] saved [the Jewish People]" can also be read as "*Vayivasha*—He was saved," and that the phrase "*Vehotzeisi eschem*—I will take you out [of Egypt]" can also be read as "*Vehutzeisi itchem*—I will be taken out along with you."

TOPPLING EVIL

This idea will explain the background to the number of *Hoshana* circuits performed over the course of the festival. On each of the first six days, we perform one circuit, while on the seventh day we circle the *bimah* seven times. This parallels the events in the very first battle that took place when we entered the Land of Israel—the battle against Jericho. There too, the people circled the city once a day for six days, and on the seventh day they circled the city seven times, at which point the walls surrounding the city crumbled.[3] In spiritual terms, we are looking to recreate this process, whereby the forces that surround evil will likewise crumble and we will be able to be redeemed from our exile.[4]

THE MOOD OF HOSHANOS

A major insight into the nature of the *Hoshanos* can be gleaned from the halachah that if a person is unfortunately in a period of mourning, they do not participate in the *Hoshanos* circuit.[5] The *Vilna Gaon* explains that the *hakafos* (circuits) in the Beis Hamikdash constituted the quintessential fulfillment of the mitzvah of "You shall rejoice before Hashem your God, for seven days,"[6] hence, a mourner cannot participate in them. This a very striking statement, and perhaps also a little

---

3   *Yerushalmi, Sukkah* 5:3.
4   See Rabbeinu Bachya, *Kad Hakemach*, s.v. "*aravah*."
5   *Rama, Orach Chaim* 660:2.
6   *Vayikra* 23:39.

unexpected. How does circling the *bimah* represent our joy during Sukkos—and its high point, no less?

Although we translate *hakafos* as "circuits" that we perform around the *bimah*, which, practically, they are, it is clearly more meaningful to relate to them as a *parade* around the *bimah*. Sukkos is a time of celebration, and *hakafos* are a celebratory parade. Although they are somewhat more formal than the dancing and merriment that takes place in the *Beis Hashoeivah* celebrations or on Simchas Torah, nevertheless, they are celebratory at heart, and hence, a person who is in mourning cannot participate in them.

This understanding of *Hoshanos* can, and should, completely change our perspective on these circuits and the atmosphere that is meant to accompany them. There tend to be many logistical considerations that occupy our minds during the *Hoshanos* circuits, beginning with confirming which *Hoshana* is the one for that day, continuing with the question of how to hold the siddur and the *arba minim* without causing damage or injury to the person in front, as well as charting a course that will effectively allow everyone to successfully circumnavigate the *bimah*! However, notwithstanding the need to handle all the above issues, how crucial it is that this not result in our losing sight of what the *Hoshanos* are all about. As we circle the *bimah* during the *Hoshanos*, we should be sure to do so with joy.

SYNERGY–FINDING A BREAKTHROUGH

Upon further reflection, the above two ideas—replicating the circuits around Jericho and expressing joy—intersect. We noted that the number of circuits over the course of Sukkos parallels those around the city of Jericho. Of course, the physical walls of Jericho are no longer of any concern to us. Which walls, then, are we looking to crumble? On a general level, we could answer that all forces of evil are fortified by walls. However, on a personal level, the walls are those that separate us from Hashem. Even after having done *teshuvah* during the *Aseres Yemei Teshuvah*, which we are confident has been accepted, and having unloaded our sins, there can still be barriers between us and Hashem. It is these we are looking to crumble. Indeed, whereas in Jericho, the walls we were looking to topple surrounded the enemy we were looking to conquer, on Sukkos, the walls surround the Torah scroll that stands at the *bimah*, and we are looking to break through them so we can embrace it completely.

The question is, with what power can we hope to crumble those walls? Are we expecting the miraculous energy that was present in Jericho to reappear and work for us here as well? Perhaps. But it appears that the energy comes from the second idea that embodies the *Hoshanos*, namely, that of the joy of performing a mitzvah before Hashem. It is with this joy that we will break through anything that stands between us and Hashem. And if we are able to do so, our personal attainment will, in its own way, be no less than those miraculous events all those years ago and, what's more, will set us on a course to see their completion.

ANI VAHO

At the conclusion of the *Hoshanos*, we say, "אני והו הושיעה נא—*Ani Vaho*, save now!" According to the Mishnah, this phrase goes back as far as the times of the Beis Hamikdash, where it would be said by the Kohanim when they circled the *Mizbeiach*.[7]

What is the meaning of "*Ani Vaho*"?

Rashi explains that these two words are actually two names of Hashem.[8] In the section leading up to the splitting of the Red Sea, there are three verses that each contain seventy-two letters:[9]

- ויסע מלאך האלקים ההלך לפני מחנה ישראל וילך מא**א**חריהם ויסע עמוד הענן מפניהם ויעמד מאחריהם.

- ויבא בין מחנה מצרים ובין מחנה ישראל ויהי הענן והחשך ויאר את הלילה ולא קרב זה אל זה כל הלילה.

- ויט משה את ידו על הים ויולך יקוק את הים ברוח קדים עזה זה כל הלילה וישם את הים לחרבה ויבקעו המים.

---

7   *Sukkah* 45a.

8   Commentary to *Sukkah* ibid.

9   *Shemos* 14:19–21.

Combining the letters from these three verses together thus gives us seventy-two three-letter names of Hashem. Specifically, the letters are combined by taking the letters of the first and third verses going forward, and from the second verse going backward. Thus, the first letter of the first verse (ו), the last of the second verse (ה) and the first of the third verse (ו) give the name "והו." The name "אני" is likewise made up from the thirty-seventh letters going forward-backward-forward (see bolded letters in the verse above).

Naturally, some questions arise:

- Why specifically were these two names "Ani" and "Vaho" chosen from the list of seventy-two?
- In the system presented by *Rashi*, the name "Vaho" is earlier than the name "Ani." Why do we mention them in the reverse order?
- Why does this system involve counting the letters of the middle verse backward? Surely, going forward is the intuitive direction, as indeed we do with the first and third verses!
- What is the significance of these names being embedded in verses leading up to the splitting of the Red Sea?
- What does any of this have to with Sukkos?

TWO OUT OF SEVENTY-TWO

In response to the first question, there is a fascinating principle propounded by the *Vilna Gaon*—which relates to numerous areas in Torah—whereby a group that consists of seventy units is also represented more generally by a set of two.[10] For example, we are aware of the concept of the seventy root nations of the world. In addition to these, we also refer to the nations of Yishmael and Eisav. These latter two are not part of the seventy;[11] rather, between them they represent all of them. Similarly, in our situation, we note that of the seventy-two names, the two that are chosen are the first and the thirty-seventh. These are the

---

10   Commentary to *Shir Hashirim* 1:2.
11   The seventy nations were established at the time of the dispersion following the episode of the Tower of Bavel (see *Bereishis*, chap. 10), many years before Yishmael and Eisav were born.

names that represent all of the seventy-two names, divided into two groups of thirty-six.[12]

Tosafos also address the question of why these two specific names were chosen.[13] They explain that this, too, relates to the theme of "the Shechinah in exile" that so pervades the *Hoshanos* service. The Midrash writes concerning two verses, (1) "ואני בתוך הגולה—And I am in the midst of the Diaspora,"[14] and (2) "והוא אסור באזקים—And he is bound in chains,"[15] that the terms *"ani"* (I) and *"hu"* (he) in those verses both refer to Hashem, saying that when the Jewish People are in exile, He is there with them and, so to speak, bound in chains.[16] Thus, we pray: "*Ani Vaho hoshiah na,*" that Hashem Who is with us in exile should redeem us and the Divine Presence along with us.

FORWARD, BACKWARD, AND FORWARD

To understand why the letters of the middle verse are counted backward, we first need to contemplate the significance of each name comprising three letters. A name of Hashem reflects the way in which He interacts with the world. Rabbeinu Bachya explains that the three letters that comprise each name correspond to the three primary attributes of *Chessed*, *Din*, and *Rachamim*—Kindness, Justice, and Mercy:[17]

- **Kindness** reflects an unqualified act of goodness on Hashem's part, regardless of whether the person merits to receive it.
- **Justice** reflects a system whereby the person receives good only if he deserves it, and likewise, receives punishment if he deserves it.
- **Mercy** constitutes a middle ground, whereby the person may not fully deserve that good, but it is nonetheless based on consideration of some merit that he has.

---

12 See *Hakesav V'Hakabbalah* to *Devarim* 29:5.
13 *Sukkah* loc. cit., s.v. "*ani*."
14 *Yechezkel* 1:1.
15 *Yirmiyahu* 40:1.
16 *Eichah Rabbasi* to *Eichah* 2:3.
17 Commentary to *Shemos* 14:21.

In Jewish mystical thought, the attribute of kindness is associated with the right side, while that of justice is associated with the left. It is for this reason that the verse from which the first letter of each name is taken, representing kindness, is read forward, for that involves starting from the right side. Conversely, the middle verse, from which the letter representing justice is taken, is read backward, for that entails starting from the left side, as is appropriate for that attribute. In light of this, we note that the third verse, representing the attribute of mercy, is also read going forward, i.e., starting from the right. This reflects the fact that although this attribute is neither pure kindness nor pure justice, it is essentially much closer to the former than the latter.

SUKKOS AND THE SPLITTING OF THE RED SEA

It is most interesting to consider the fact that the two names that become so central in the *Hoshanos* on Sukkos are rooted in the verses leading up to the splitting of the Red Sea. Indeed, as we ponder these two things, we can begin to see how connected they are:

Sukkos is the time when we are judged concerning water for the coming year. Our very first judgment as a people regarding water took place at the Red Sea, when we were judged as to whether we were worthy to have the sea split for us and stay open as we passed through. The Midrash relates that the Attribute of Justice charged that we were guilty of many sins and were not deserving of such a miracle. However, in the end, Hashem had mercy on us, ascribing our misdeeds to external circumstances and pressures. Thus, as we are being judged on Sukkos, we invoke names that were revealed at the splitting of the Red Sea, asking Hashem to have mercy on us now in our judgment regarding water as He did then.

In this regard, it is fascinating to note that throughout the course of the Chumash, the Torah uses various terms with which to refer to the redemption: "והוצאתי—I will take [you] out," "והצלתי—I will save you," "וגאלתי—I will deliver you," "הפודך—[the One] Who redeemed you."

There is only one instance where a different term is used to denote salvation, and that is at the event of the splitting of the Red Sea: "ויושע ה' ביום ההוא את ישראל מיד מצרים—Hashem saved Israel on that day from the hand of Egypt." Hashem's salvation at the Splitting of the Sea is associated with the specific term "*Vayosha*," the very term that is the motif of the "*Hoshana*" service on Sukkos.

The splitting of the Red Sea also relates to the theme of Sukkos, generally. Sukkos commemorates the *Ananei Hakavod* with which Hashem surrounded and protected us in the *midbar*. The first time we see Hashem's cloud act in a protective (i.e., not only guiding) capacity is described in the very verses from which the seventy-two names are derived:[18] Hashem moved the cloud from being in front of the Jewish People to behind them, thereby plunging the Egyptians into complete darkness and slowing down their advance, as well as absorbing any arrows or missiles they tried to launch against the Jewish People.[19]

Sukkos, the Red Sea, and Hidur Mitzvah

A major connecting point between Sukkos and the Splitting of the Sea that impacts on the realm of mitzvah observance is *hidur mitzvah*—beautifying a mitzvah. This concept features centrally in the *arba minim* on Sukkos, with the *esrog* itself being identified as "*hadar*—beautiful." The source in the Torah for the general concept of *hidur mitzvah* is derived from a verse in *Az Yashir*, the song we sang after passing through the Red Sea, which states, "זה א-לי ואנוהו"—This is my God and I will glorify Him,"[20] as the Gemara expounds: "התנאה לפניו במצוות"—Beautify yourself before Him with mitzvos."[21]

Hidur mitzvah represents the desire to go beyond the basic fulfillment of the mitzvah. What would motivate the Jewish People to start thinking in this direction? It was Hashem who made the first move, showing His love and protection for His people through the *Ananei Hakavod*, which went beyond providing for their basic needs through such items such as the manna and Miriam's well. When contemplating what lies behind those gestures from Above, the people themselves responded by thinking how they, too, could put special care and love into their mitzvos through adorning and beautifying them.

---

18   *Shemos* 14:19–20.
19   See *Rashi* ibid.
20   Ibid., 15:2.
21   *Shabbos* 133a.

RAMBAM: CALLING ON SALVATION

Thus far, we have discussed the term *"Ani Vaho"* as denoting two names of Hashem. A very different approach to this term can be found in the *Rambam's* Commentary to the Mishnah:

> I say that they are calling out to the One Who said, "אני אני הוא—I, I am He,"[22] a verse which was said concerning the victory and salvation of Israel. As if to say, "You, the One Who says, 'See now that I, I am He [אני אני הוא],' save us now, as You have promised us."[23]

This approach will help explain a basic question regarding the phrase *"Ani Vaho,"* namely, the order of the two terms. If they are names of Hashem, Why is the earlier name *"Vaho"* mentioned second and the later name *"Ani"* mentioned first? According to the *Rambam's* explanation, the matter is understood, as this is the order that the two words appear in the verse, *"Ani Hu."*

HARMONY

However, while the *Rambam* himself presents his approach that the words *"Ani Vaho"* refer to the verse in *Devarim* as an alternative to the idea that they refer to names of Hashem, other commentators explain that those words in *Devarim* are themselves also associated with the two names of *"Ani Vaho."* Thus, Rabbeinu Bachya, in his commentary to *Devarim* writes:

> These words ["Ani" and "Hu"] are both Divine names, as we say, "Ani Vaho hoshiah na."

How are we to understand the presence of the two names *"Ani Vaho"* in that verse in *Devarim*?

The verse in question is at the end of *Parshas Haazinu*, which foretells the history of the Jewish People. The verse states that when history

---

22   *Devarim* 32:39.

23   *Sukkah* 4:5.

has run its course, the people will realize that it was Hashem Who had guided their experiences throughout their exiles. In this context, the two names "*Ani*" and "*Vaho*" are referenced. To understand the full significance of their presence in that verse, we need to discover one more thing about these two names.

One of the great scholars among the Acharonim, R' Wolf Heidenheim, explains that the two names "*Ani*" and "*Vaho*" are themselves abridged representations of the two names *Adnus* and *Havayah*.[24] As we have discussed in an earlier chapter, these two names represent Hashem as the Controller of the world and its Creator, respectively. As such, the verse is saying that in the future, we will see how although our national experiences through history took place within the natural frame of world events—events that were at times baffling, confusing, and even heartbreaking and distressing—it was Hashem Who was overseeing those natural events and experiences (*Ani*), the very same Hashem Who created the world and its nature in the first place (*Vaho*).

As we have seen, this idea is one of the core themes of Sukkos: looking at one's harvest that has been produced through natural agricultural means and processes, and seeing behind it the hand of the One Who provided the *Ananei Hakavod* for us in the *midbar*.

REALITY AND RECOGNITION

With this, perhaps we can now understand why the order of the names "*Ani Vaho*" as we call upon them is the opposite of the order in which they appear in the verse. For while in terms of reality, Hashem as Creator (*Vaho*) of the world will then guide its nature (*Ani*), from the point of view of our perception, the order is reversed: first we look at the world around us and see it as being guided by Hashem (*Ani*), and from there we perceive Hashem as the Creator (*Vaho*) behind it all. In the merit of this recognition, we call upon Hashem to save us and bring us to the point where our entire history will receive full perspective and understanding: "אני והו הושיעה נא"!

---

24   Cited in *Siddur Otzar Hatefillos, Hoshanos*.

CHAPTER 14

THE TORAH READING

The Torah reading for the first day of Sukkos (in the Diaspora, the first two days) is chapter 23 of *Chumash Vayikra*, which discusses all the festivals of the Jewish year. For purposes of this volume, it is worthwhile contemplating—through the medium of the classic commentators—aspects of the Torah reading that relate to Yom Tov in general and the festival of Sukkos specifically.

PART I: YOM TOV

WHY DO WE START WITH "SHOR O KESEV"?

The first question to consider is somewhat surprising, as it relates not to something *that* we read on this day, but to the more basic question of *why* we do so. Although, as we mentioned, the Torah reading mainly comprises chapter 23 of *Vayikra*, it actually begins with the final few verses of chapter 22. These verses contain mitzvos that apply to any day of the year, such as the prohibition against slaughtering an animal and its offspring on the same day, the laws of the *todah* offering, and the prohibition against desecrating Hashem name. After that, we proceed to the chapter that discusses the festivals. The question, of course, is why do we open the reading with the above-mentioned verses? Why not simply start the reading with the festivals themselves in chapter 23?

The *Netziv* explains that while these commandments are indeed applicable on any day of the year, they have special significance around the time of Yom Tov.[1]

Some examples:

- **Slaughtering an animal and its offspring**: While the prohibition against slaughtering an animal and its offspring on the same day applies throughout the year, this is of particular concern around the time of the festivals, where many animals will be brought as offerings.
- **The *Todah* offering**: Regarding the verses concerning the *todah* offering, the matter is more difficult, as these laws have actually *already been stated in full* earlier in *Chumash Vayikra*! The reason they are repeated here is that they relate specifically to a thanksgiving offering that one would bring during the festival. During the year, one brings such an offering in response to a specific miracle or kindness that Hashem performed for him. This would motivate him to take the trip to the Beis Hamikdash and offer a *todah*. During the festivals, however, when one is in any case in the environs of the Beis Hamikdash, he might feel inspired to bring a *todah*, not in response to something in particular, but as a general expression of appreciation for the kindness Hashem bestows upon him all year round. It is this *todah* that is discussed in our parsha—the section dealing with the *Moadim*.

  Indeed, the differing nature of this *todah* requires the Torah to reiterate here the laws governing the consumption of the *korban*. The time frame the Torah normally allows for a *todah* is just one day. The reason for this is that since it is forbidden to leave consecrated food unconsumed past its allotted time, the shortened time frame will encourage the person to invite others to share his

---

1   *Haamek Davar* to *Vayikra* ibid.

korban with them. This will give him the opportunity to relate to them the reason he brought the *korban*—giving greater glory to Hashem by publicizing the miracle. As such, when it comes to a *todah* that he brings with no particular incident in mind, we might have thought that the time frame would revert to the standard two days that are allowed for *korbanos* of this category. To this end, the Torah emphasizes that even this *korban* must be consumed over the course of one day only.

• **The prohibition against profaning Hashem's name**: Here, too, although this prohibition is applicable throughout the year, it is of particular relevance on the festivals, where there is a concern that the joyous atmosphere that accompanies the day may lead to levity and inappropriate conduct.

And thus, without adding any words of elaboration, the very inclusion of these verses in the Torah reading of the festivals encourages us to discern their relevance to these days.[2]

INTRODUCING THE FESTIVALS WITH SHABBOS

אלה הם מועדי. ששת ימים תעשה מלאכה וביום השביעי שבת.

These are My festivals. For six days, labor shall be performed, and on the seventh day, Shabbos.[3]

There appears to be a digression in these opening verses. The first verse very noticeably starts by introducing the festivals, yet the next verse immediately veers off to talk about Shabbos before returning in the ensuing verses to the festivals themselves! Commenting on this phenomenon, the Midrash, cited by *Rashi*, states that it is to teach us that anyone who violates the festivals is considered as if he has violated the Shabbos. What is the meaning behind the equation of these two days, such that violating one is like violating the other?

---

2   See *Haamek Davar* there for a similar explanation of the other mitzvos contained within these verses.

3   *Vayikra* 23:2–3.

R' Moshe Feinstein explains.[4] Shabbos acknowledges Hashem as Creator of the world. However, there are those who subscribe to the concept of Hashem as Creator but do not recognize His ongoing involvement in the world past that point. Yet, significantly, this approach is deficient even in terms of its belief in Creation itself, for it fails to see the purpose within that very Creation—something that involves Hashem's guidance of history and the revelation of His will through the Jewish People. It is these concepts that are reflected by the festivals. Thus, one who violates the festivals, expressing thereby his refusal to embrace an awareness of Hashem's role in history and His purpose for the world, is considered as if he violated Shabbos—as his notion of the Creation that is marked by Shabbos is impaired and, ultimately, devoid of meaning.

PART II: SUKKOS

THE TORAH'S TWO PRESENTATIONS OF SUKKOS

When surveying the Torah's presentation of the various festivals of the year, the festival of Sukkos stands out in that it is presented twice. The Torah initially introduces Sukkos in verse 34: "On the fifteenth day of the seventh month…" and then it does so again in verse 39 before presenting the mitzvos of the festival: "However, on the fifteenth day of the seventh month…" What is behind this double presentation?

The *Chasam Sofer* explains that these two distinct presentations reflect the two aspects of the festival of Sukkos itself.[5] As we discussed in an earlier chapter, Sukkos is not only the culmination of the *Regalim*, it is also the culmination of the *Yamim Noraim*.

- The first presentation, which comes directly after Rosh Hashanah and Yom Kippur, discusses Sukkos as the last of the *Yamim Noraim*. Accordingly, its timing is introduced generally as "the fifteenth day of the seventh month."

---

4   *Darash Moshe.*
5   *Parshas Haazinu.*

- The second presentation reflects Sukkos as the last of the *Regalim*, hence, it is introduced with the words, "On the fifteenth day of the seventh month, when you gather in the produce of the land," accentuating the agricultural element that applies to the *Regalim*.[6]

THE FOUR SPECIES–IN THE VERSE AND IN THE MITZVAH

In terms of the basic mitzvah, the *arba minim* do not need to be in any way attached to each other. However, as a beautification of the mitzvah, they are bound together. Specifically, the *lulav*, *hadasim*, and *aravos* are bound together, while the *esrog* is held together with them, but not bound with them. Interestingly, this arrangement is alluded to in the verse that presents the *arba minim*, which describes them as follows:

פרי עץ הדר כפת תמרים וענף עץ עבת וערבי נחל.

The fruit of a citron tree, the branches of date-palms and twigs of plaited tree and willows of the stream.[7]

As a rule, when the Torah lists more than one item, it only places a *vav* prior to mentioning the last item. A simple example of this is the verse in the beginning of *Chumash Shemos*,[8] "ראובן שמעון לוי ויהודה." Conveniently, this formulation is reflected in the English translation, which also typically only has the word "and" before the final item, as in this case, "Reuven, Shimon, Levi, and Yehudah." In our verse, by contrast, in addition to before the fourth item (the *aravos*—וערבי נחל) there is also a *vav* between the second and third items (*lulav* and

---

6   In a similar vein, other commentators explain the division of Sukkos into the command-ments that were applicable in the *midbar*, such as observing the day as Yom Tov and offering *korbanos*, and those that would only apply once they had entered the land, such as the mitzvos of sukkah and the *arba minim*. This would seem especially appropriate in light of the idea that the latter two mitzvos are, in fact, a celebration of entering the land (responsa *Tzitz Eliezer*, vol. 7, sec. 31).

7   *Vayikra* 23:39.

8   1:2.

hadasim—עבת עץ וענף תמרים כפת). The only place where there is no *vav* is between the *esrog* and the *lulav*. The letter *vav*, as we know, serves to connect. Thus, the verse alludes to the idea that even when all four species are taken together, the final three are more connected with each other, being bound together, while the *esrog* remains somewhat distinct and is not bound together with them.[9]

Taking Note of Taamei Hamikra

Although the enhanced manner of performing the mitzvah involves binding the species together, as far as the pure halachah is concerned, the *Shulchan Aruch* rules that the *arba minim* do not even need to be taken at the same time; they can be taken one at a time. The only proviso is that all four species need to be present before the person when he takes them, even though he then takes them one after the other.[10]

There is a tradition from the *Vilna Gaon* that the *taamei hamikra* (cantillation notes) that accompany the words in the Chumash can also serve as commentary to those words.[11] Here, too, the *taamim* accompanying the words "ולקחתם לכם" are known as *kadma ve'azla*. The word *"kadma"* means before, while *"azla"* means to go. The notes accompanying the words "ביום הראשון" are called *munach revii*. *"Munach"* means placed and *"revii"* means the fourth. Putting this all together, the *taamim* on top of the words that command us to take the species are telling us that we can take them in a manner that is *"kadma ve'azla,"* one goes before the other, i.e., not at the same time, provided that they are *"munach revii,"* i.e., all four of them are placed before the person at the time.

PRI EITZ HADAR

The first of the *arba minim* to be mentioned in the verse is *"pri eitz hadar."* The word *hadar* means "beauty" and this phrase thus refers to the *esrog*. Most intriguingly, although the matter would seem to be as

---

9   *Toras Kohanim*, as explained by R' Baruch Halevi Epstein (author of *Torah Temimah*) in *Tosefes Berachah* to *Vayikra* loc. cit.

10   *Orach Chaim* 651:12.

11   See, for example, *Kol Eliyahu*, beginning of *Parshas Vayigash*.

simple as that, *Rashi* cites two somewhat more elaborate explanations of this term:

- The taste of the fruit and the tree is identical. This interpretation derives from seeing the words "*pri*" and "*eitz*" as being equated with each other.
- The fruit stays on the tree from one year to the next. This interpretation explains the word "*hadar*" not as "beauty," but as "that which lives [*dar*]," with the *hei* (**ha**dar) serving as a prefix to denote the definite article.

This matter is quite perplexing. *Rashi*'s goal is to offer, wherever possible, the *pshat* meaning of the words. In our case, seeing as the *pshat* meaning seemingly couldn't be clearer, Why does *Rashi* give entry to expositions that clearly do not belong to the realm of *pshat*?

In truth, however, *Rashi* is addressing a basic and disarmingly simple question regarding these words. The literal translation of "*pri eitz hadar*" is "the fruit of a beautiful tree." Now, the beauty of the *esrog* tree lies in the fact that it produces beautiful fruit. As such, since we are discussing the fruit, the verse's description of "the fruit of a beautiful tree" seems to be somewhat roundabout, for why not simply describe the *esrog* as "*pri hadar*—a beautiful fruit"? In response to this *pshat* question, *Rashi* cites the above two explanations, for each of them addresses the inclusion of the word "tree" in the Torah's description:

- The taste of the fruit is like that of the tree.
- The fruit stays on the tree from one year to the next.[12]

THE MEANING OF THE WORD "SUKKOS"

After presenting the mitzvah of dwelling in sukkos, the Torah provides the reason for the mitzvah:

---

12   In this instance, the *drash* exposition actually leads us back to the *pshat* of the phrase. The reason the *esrog* tree is called "*eitz hadar*" is by virtue of the beautiful fruit that adorns it on an ongoing basis as it stays on the tree from one year to the next (R' Leib Mintzberg, *Ben Melech, Sukkos*, chap. 5).

למען ידעו דרתיכם כי בסכות הושבתי את בני ישראל בהוציאי אותם מארץ
מצרים.

*In order that your generations will know that I caused them
to dwell in sukkos when I took them out of the land of Egypt.*[13]

As we have discussed in earlier chapters, there is a dispute among the Tannaim regarding which "sukkos" we are commemorating. According to Rabbi Akiva, it is the actual huts in which we dwelled, while according to Rabbi Eliezer it is the *Ananei Hakavod* that surrounded us. It is very interesting to note that *Rashi*, in his commentary to our verse, explains "sukkos" in accordance with Rabbi Eliezer's view, namely, that we recall the *Ananei Hakavod*! This is most remarkable, since *Rashi*'s goal in his commentary on the Torah is to present, wherever possible, the straightforward meaning of the verse. Surely, between the two available explanations of either clouds or huts, huts should be considered the *pshat*!

Rabbeinu Eliyahu Mizrachi, foremost among the commentators on *Rashi*, explains that a closer look at the phraseology of the verse will indicate it is actually the explanation of "sukkos" as clouds that is the *pshat*. The term with which the Torah describes our dwelling in those sukkos is "הושבתי—I caused to dwell." This word implies that our dwelling in sukkos was something that Hashem caused, and not something that we did by ourselves. Hence, *Rashi* explains the verse as referring to the *Ananei Hakavod*, something that only Hashem could bring about![14]

THE MITZVAH OF SUKKAH: A CHOK–AND TWO REASONS

חקת עולם...תחגו...בסכת תשבו...כל האזרח בישראל ישבו בסכת. למען
ידעו דרתיכם כי בסכות הושבתי את־בני ישראל בהוציאי אותם מארץ
מצרים.

---

13   *Vayikra* 23:43.

14   Also noteworthy is that *Onkelos* to our verse likewise translates "sukkos" as "במטללות
עננא—in the shade of clouds," in accordance with the view of Rabbi Eliezer. (See *Megillah* 3a, where it records that *Onkelos* was a student of Rabbi Eliezer. In numerous instances such as ours, commentators point out how *Onkelos*'s translation reflects the approach of Rabbi Eliezer, his teacher.)

An eternal decree for your generations...you shall dwell in sukkos for seven days, every native in Israel shall dwell in sukkos. In order that your generations will know that I caused the Children of Israel to dwell in sukkos when I took them from the land of Egypt.[15]

Our verses appear to contain a contradiction. On the one hand, the mitzvah of dwelling in sukkos is presented as a *"chukas olam."* The term *chok* generally denotes a mitzvah whose reason is not known to us. Yet, having said that, the ensuing verses proceed to provide the reason for the mitzvah, "so that your generations will know, etc."

The *Netziv* explains that the term *chok* in our verse does not mean to imply that the reason for the mitzvah is not known.[16] Rather, it is to establish that the mitzvah is fixed for all time, regardless of whether any particular reason applies at that time. For in fact, there is more than one reason for the mitzvah, and it is something that can change almost from one extreme to the other, depending on the state of the Jewish People.

- When the people are in their land, this is the season when they "gather in the harvest of the land." At this time, as we have seen, they might be prone to become overly confident in their own prowess, leading to complacency and to forgetting Hashem, the Source of their blessing and success. To this end, the Torah requires us to dwell in sukkos for seven days, so that we recall the transient nature of our existence and our dependence on Hashem. In this regard, the Torah states that "every native in the land," i.e., those who feel that their presence in the land is immutable, "shall dwell in sukkos."
- When the Jewish People are in exile, they may not be bringing in the harvest in the country in which they sojourn. In these times, they will naturally feel that their existence is precarious.

---

15   *Vayikra* 23:41–43.

16   *Drashah* given on the occasion of the dedication of the new *beis midrash* building in Volozhin, Chol Hamoed Sukkos 1860, cited in *Drashos HaNetziv*, sec. 8.

In these periods, the Torah commands to dwell in sukkos for the opposite reason: to recall how, even when we were in the *midbar*, we were surrounded by Hashem's Divine protection, "So that your generations may know that I caused the Children of Israel to dwell in sukkos when I took them out the land of Egypt."

And thus, the mitzvah of sukkos itself is everlasting and constant—"*chukas olam.*" It is not beholden to any one reason, but rather, the same mitzvah reflects different themes at different stages in our history, as the ensuing verses proceed to outline.

THE MITZVAH OF SUKKAH AND THE EXODUS FROM EGYPT

בסכת תשבו שבעת ימים...למען ידעו דרתיכם כי בסכות הושבתי את בני ישראל בהוציאי אותם מארץ מצרים.

You shall dwell in sukkos for seven days...In order that your generations will know that I caused the Children of Israel to dwell in sukkos when I took them out of the land of Egypt.[17]

It is interesting to note that out of all the festivals mentioned in this chapter, the only one that has the Exodus from Egypt explicitly mentioned in connection with it is Sukkos! The *Meshech Chochmah* explains that the full meaning and realization of the Exodus is the idea that once Hashem delivered us from slavery to become His servants, we can never entirely be in servitude to anyone else.[18] Thus, for example, the Torah concludes its discussion of the laws of *eved ivri* (the Hebrew servant) by saying, "כי עבדי הם—For they are My servants,"[19] which the Gemara expounds upon as "ולא עבדים לעבדים—and not servants to [other] servants."[20] In other words, as a consequence of the Exodus, the servitude of a Jew to anyone other than Hashem can never be a permanent state.

---

17   *Vayikra* 23:42–43.
18   *Meshech Chochmah* to ibid.
19   *Vayikra* 25:55.
20   *Bava Metzia* 10a.

Likewise, on a national level, the basis of the assurance that Hashem will ultimately redeem the Jewish People from its subjugation to other nations in subsequent exiles is the Exodus from Egypt. Hence, the verse at the end of *Chumash Vayikra* that discusses the exile the Jewish People could incur as a result of ignoring the mitzvos, and which foretells of their redemption from that exile, states: "וזכרתי להם ברית ראשנים אשר הוצאתי אתם מארץ מצרים...להית להם לאלקים—I will remember for them the covenant of the earlier ones, whom I took out of Egypt...to be a God unto them."[21]

The means through which our exclusive connection with Hashem is "activated" is through keeping the mitzvos, which serve to sanctify our physical existence and place us within His protective domain. Almost all mitzvos relate to one part of the body only. An exception to this rule is the mitzvah of appearing before Hashem in the Beis Hamikdash during the *Shalosh Regalim*, which is done with the entire body. However, even there, while the entire physical body is involved in the mitzvah, physical existence itself is not, for there is no eating or drinking allowed while performing this mitzvah. The ultimate example of a mitzvah that involves the entire body is that of sukkah, where not only does the person enter the sukkah, but his physical existence enters with it, eating, drinking, and sleeping in the sukkah. Indeed, the sukkah commemorates the *Ananei Hakavod*, which likewise enveloped our entire existence while we were in the *midbar*.

We can now understand why, out of the entire section dealing with the *Moadim*, it is specifically in connection with the festival of Sukkos that the Exodus from Egypt receives explicit mention. For the mitzvah of sukkah embraces and sanctifies the totality of physical existence, thereby affirming and empowering our connection with Hashem that was initiated when He took us out of Egypt and giving full realization to the concept of the Exodus from there.

---

21   *Vayikra* 26:45.

ORDINANCE AND EXPERIENCE—THE LAWS OF THE FESTIVAL ON THE FESTIVAL

The concluding verse of the Torah reading says:

וידבר משה את מעדי ה' אל בני ישראל.

And Moshe spoke the festivals of Hashem to the Children of Israel.[22]

Commenting on this verse, the Gemara states that Moshe instituted that the Jewish People occupy themselves with "הלכות חג בחג—the halachos of a festival on that festival."[23] On the face of it, the goal of this study is easily understood: they are to review the laws that are relevant to that festival in order to ensure that they observe them properly. However, the commentators raise a simple question: There are numerous laws pertaining to the festivals where reviewing the relevant laws on the festival itself would be too late. For example, what if a person discovers that their sukkah is halachically disqualified? They can't build a new one on Yom Tov; neither can they pick new species in the event that the ones they have chosen are problematic. These are things that one would specifically want to know *before* the festival, not on it!

Indeed, the Gemara elsewhere informs us of a parallel enactment of reviewing the halachos of a festival beginning thirty days prior to the festival.[24] How does that enactment relate to the enactment of Moshe? Has it supplanted or replaced it?[25]

Perhaps we can perceive an element within Moshe's enactment that can only be fulfilled on the festival itself. In the blessing of *Ahavah Rabbah* that we recite before *Shema* each morning, we beseech Hashem for assistance in the study of His Torah: "And place within our hearts...to listen, learn, and teach, to guard, and perform all the words of Your Torah with love." Having concluded that series of requests, we immediately continue, "Illuminate our eyes in Your Torah." What is the

---

22 *Vayikra* 23:44.
23 *Megillah* 32a.
24 *Pesachim* 6.
25 See *Beis Yosef, Orach Chaim* 429, who raises and discusses this question.

meaning of this second request for Torah illumination? What does it add to the initial petition that Hashem place within our hearts to learn His Torah?

R' Shmuel Halevi Wosner explains that these two requests reflect two different stages.[26] The first request relates to the learning one does that leads and enables him to perform the mitzvos. However, once a person actually performs the mitzvah, a new level of understanding becomes possible. Man is a composite being, comprised of both physical and spiritual elements that affect each other. For example, a person's ability to focus on and understand an idea can be directly affected by how awake and healthy they are physically. Hence, prior to fulfilling the mitzvah, only the spiritual and intellectual part of the person is involved. However, once the person has actually fulfilled the mitzvah, all aspects of his being are now connected to it, which can then allow for a further level of illumination regarding the mitzvah itself. And thus, after having requested assistance in learning the mitzvah through to its performance, we follow up with a request that is only possible at that stage: "Illuminate our eyes in Your Torah."

Similarly, although there are days set aside leading up to the festival devoted to learning the relevant laws with a view to attaining practical fluency and proficiency, there is a second enactment reserved for the festival itself. At this time, when our entire being is immersed in the experience of the festival and involved in the performance of its laws, that immersion can lead to a higher understanding of those laws—one that is available only on the festival itself.

---

26   *Drashos Shevet Halevi*, p. 96.

CHAPTER 15

KOHELES

INTRODUCTION: FOR EACH SCROLL A TIME

On the Shabbos of Chol Hamoed Sukkos, the custom is to read the book of *Koheles* in shul just before the Torah reading.[1] In fact, the connection between *Koheles* and Sukkos predates this custom by many centuries. The *Avudraham* cites a tradition that the contents of the book of *Koheles* were originally communicated by Shlomo Hamelech to the people in the form of sermons he gave before the masses on Sukkos itself.

Indeed, this idea relates to the very meaning of the name *Koheles*, which Shlomo used for this book. The word "*koheles*" derives from the word "*kahal*," which means "assembly." Some suggest that this name reflects the fact that Shlomo had, through experience and contemplation, assembled all forms of wisdom available in the world. Others, however, explain that it expresses the idea that he gave these teachings over to all those who were assembled before him on Sukkos.[2]

The *Ramban*[3] writes that present at these discourses were also many people from among the nations of the world, and it is concerning

---

1   In a year where there is no Shabbos during Chol Hamoed, *Koheles* is read in Eretz Yisrael on the first day of Sukkos, and in the Diaspora on Shemini Atzeres.
2   See *Rashi* to verse 1.
3   *Drashah* on *Koheles*.

these sermons that the verse states, "ויבאו מכל העמים לשמוע את חכמת
שלמה—People came from all the nations to hear the wisdom of Shlomo."[4]
Hence, the content and discourse in *Koheles*, while primarily addressed
to the Jewish People, is not restricted to them in the sense that it discusses themes that are relevant and compelling to anyone who wishes
to live a meaningful existence.[5]

KOHELES, VANITY–AND JOY?

Upon initial consideration, the theme of this book does not seem
entirely appropriate for Sukkos. After all, Sukkos is "the time of our
joy," while *Koheles* declares everything to be vain and futile! However,
upon further reflection, the message of *Koheles* is indeed in keeping
with that of the festival. As the Gemara points out, *Koheles* states that
there is no enduring meaning or happiness from endeavors that are
"under the sun,"[6] i.e., temporal in nature. Things that are "above the
sun," however, i.e., spiritual endeavors, are indeed the source of lasting
joy and fulfillment, and it is to them that a person should direct his
main focus and energies.[7] As *Koheles* concludes at the end of the final
chapter: "The sum of the matter, when all has been considered: Fear
God and keep His commandments, for this is all of man."[8]

As we have seen, this is the very message of Sukkos. At the very time
of our joy, the Torah commands that our physical dwelling be temporary
in nature, with the *schach* on its top coming from the relatively unim-
portant elements of the harvest. This reflects the idea that all physical

---

4   *Melachim I* 5:14. Putting the above two ideas together, the *Netziv* (*Haamek Davar* to *Bamidbar*
    29:12) writes that emissaries of the nations of the world would visit Jerusalem particularly
    on Sukkos—as indeed the Navi Zecharyah (14:17) prophesies they will in the future—since
    korbanos were offered at that time on their behalf. Hence, they would be present at the
    sermons that Shlomo would deliver to the public on Sukkos.
5   For this reason, throughout *Koheles*, Hashem is referred to only as *Elokim*, and not with the
    Shem Havayah, since the latter name is meaningful only to the Jewish People, who enjoy
    a special relationship with Him, while *Elokim* refers to Him as God in a way that is accessible
    to all (*Netziv* ibid.).
6   1:3.
7   *Shabbos* 30b.
8   12:13.

pursuits are secondary to more meaningful goals. Thus, *Koheles* is, in a sense, the handbook for discovering where to search in pursuit of true happiness. Although a full study of *Koheles* would naturally require its own volume, below are a selection of comments on verses in *Koheles* that highlight the above theme.

FROM KOHELES

הבל הבלים אמר קהלת:

"Havel havalim," says Koheles.

Rashi translates the words *"havel havalim"* as, "vanity of vanities," so that the word *"havel"* is a construct word, i.e., *"hevel* of."[9] However, the *Ramban* explains[10] that the word *"havel"* is in the grammatical form of a command.[11] As such, the verse is not *issuing a pronouncement* about the nature of the world, to say that it is vanity, but rather, it is *giving an instruction* to ensure that one recognizes and treats as vanity that which is so.

Additionally, the word *"hevel"* itself, which we commonly translate as "vanity," is explained by the *Ramban* as being associated with the word *"hevel"* as vapor, i.e., something that is insubstantial and transient. Accordingly, *Koheles* opens by adjuring us to recognize that which is transient in life and that which is enduring and meaningful. With our perspective on these two areas set, we can then proceed to eschew the former and embrace and develop the latter.

טוב מלא כף נחת ממלא חפנים עמל ורעות רוח:

Better is one handful of pleasantness than two fistfuls of labor and broken spirit.[12]

---

9   Like *"chalev imo*—the milk of its mother" (*Shemos* 23:19).
10   *Drashah* on *Koheles.*
11   Like *kadesh* (sanctify) or *aseh* (do).
12   4:6.

On the face of it, this verse appears difficult in the sense that it is completely obvious: surely *any* amount of something good is better than *any* amount of something bad, and how much more so it is better than a larger amount of something bad!

The common notion regarding *Koheles* is that he (i.e., Shlomo Hamelech) negates everything in the world, dubbing it "vanity." However, as we have seen, that is not entirely accurate. *Koheles* urges us not to lay primary emphasis on matters of this world for their own sake, rather, as a setting for attaining higher pursuits. If a person maintains this perspective, he will engage in the world in moderation, represented by taking "one handful" of pleasure from the world, and *this itself* is what will give him pleasure from the world. It is only when a person begins to prioritize matters of this world, viewing them as the sum total of his aspirations, as represented by trying to attain "two fistfuls," that the entire enterprise then yields only frustration and a broken spirit.[13]

סוף דבר הכל נשמע את האלקים ירא ואת מצותיו שמור כי זה כל האדם. כי את כל מעשה האלקים יבא במשפט על כל נעלם אם טוב ואם רע:

The sum of the matter, when all has been considered: Fear God and keep His commandments, for this is all of man. For God will judge each deed, concerning every hidden thing, whether good or evil.[14]

Having established that fear of Heaven and keeping mitzvos are the only truly worthwhile endeavors, to what "hidden thing" is the final verse referring to, stating that it will be judged by Hashem?

The *Kesav Sofer* explains that the book of *Koheles* opens by declaring that all of man's toil in matters of this world are *hevel*—vain and devoid of meaning. However, there is an important caveat here. Fulfilling Torah and mitzvos is of ultimate value, and doing so is made possible by toiling in matters of this world. A person needs food, sleep, shelter, and

---

13   *Ramban* loc. cit., p. 191 in Mossad Harav Kook ed.
14   12:13–14.

a livelihood in order to function—including regarding elevated endeavors. Surely, this then bestows on those activities an aspect of meaning!

Indeed, when *Koheles* initially negates the benefit of man's toil in this world, he says, "מה יתרון לאדם בכל עמלו שיעמל תחת השמש—What benefit does man have from all his toil which he toils under the sun." The word "שיעמל—which he toils," seems redundant, for surely the preceding word, "עמלו—his toil," is none other than "that which he toils"!

Rather, the point is that man's toil in temporal matters is meaningless if all that toil is only "that he will toil," i.e., purely directed toward further toil, with no higher goal in sight. However, if he engages in those very same endeavors with the intention for them to serve as the basis for higher living, then they too become infused with higher meaning. This, however, is entirely dependent on a person's intentions, which are concealed within. Therefore, *Koheles* concludes by saying two things:

- Fear of God and keeping mitzvos are the only things of essential ultimate value in this world.
- Hashem will judge a person in terms of that which is concealed within them, regarding whether they engaged in matters of this world for elevated reasons, thereby bestowing upon these matters essential meaning.

SUKKOS IN THE BEIS HAMIKDASH

CHAPTER 16

THE KORBANOS OF SUKKOS

In addition to its unique mitzvos, the festival of Sukkos is also distinguished by the special *korbanos* that are offered in the Beis Hamikdash as its additional *mussaf* offerings. Although we are not currently able to offer the *korbanos* in practice, nevertheless, pondering their themes and particulars will yield messages that can serve to illuminate the festival—and the year beyond.

THE SEVENTY BULLS, PART I: LESS IS MORE

One of the well-known distinctive aspects of the offerings of Sukkos are the seventy bulls that are brought over the course of the seven days. The Gemara explains the significance of these offerings:

> הני שבעים פרים כנגד מי? כנגד שבעים אומות...אמר רבי יוחנן, אוי להם
> לעובדי כוכבים שאבדו ואין יודעין מה שאבדו, בזמן שבית המקדש קיים
> מזבח מכפר עליהם, ועכשיו מי מכפר עליהן?

> *To whom do these seventy bulls correspond? To the seventy nations [of the world]...Said Rabbi Yochanan, "Woe to the idol worshippers who have lost and do not know what they have lost! As long as the Beis Hamikdash was standing, the Mizbeiach atoned for them; now, who will atone for them?"[1]*

---

1   *Sukkah 55b.*

We see that these offerings are brought on behalf of the entire population of the world, to atone for them and provide for their well-being. The Gemara continues that the seventy bulls offered on Sukkos are contrasted with the one bull that is offered on Shemini Atzeres, which reflects the special relationship the Jewish People enjoy with Hashem. As the Gemara expresses it: "This can be compared to a king who told his servants to prepare a great feast. On the final day, he said to his close friend, 'Prepare a small [i.e., private] feast for me so that I may enjoy your company.'"

Effectively, what the combination of these offerings represents is the good will that the Jewish People have for the nations of the world generally, alongside—and as part of—their special status as Hashem's people.

A View from Afar

According to the *Vilna Gaon*, this idea is alluded to in *Parshas Vayeira*, in which our Patriarch, Avraham, steps forward to pray for the people of Sodom.[2] For even though they are not members of his family or group, and their actions and beliefs are, moreover, antithetical to his moral principles and teachings, nevertheless he is prepared to ask for mercy for them. As a preamble to his pleas on their behalf, he states, "ואנכי עפר ואפר—And I am dust and ashes."[3] On a straightforward level, these are words of self-deprecation, whereby Avraham is saying, "I wish to pray for them, *although* I am dust and ashes." However, there is also an allusion in these words, whereby Avraham is saying, "I wish to pray for them *because* I am dust and ashes." How is this so?

- The word "עפר" comprises the letters "ע-פר," denoting "seventy cows," as פר means bull and the letter ע has the numerical value of seventy.
- The word "אפר," comprises the letters "א-פר," denoting one bull, as the numerical value of א is one.

---

2   Cited by R' Avraham Korman, *Haparshah L'Doroseha*.
3   *Bereishis* 18:27.

> Thus, Avraham is saying, "Since I embody the message of the seventy bulls (ע-פר) along with the one bull (א-פר), I wish to pray even for the people of Sodom."

Notably, these seventy bulls are not brought in a uniform way, i.e., ten bulls per day. Rather they are brought in decreasing order, with thirteen being offered on the first day, twelve on the second and so on until seven bulls are offered on the seventh day. Commenting on this descending order, *Rashi*, citing the Midrash, writes:

פרי החג שבעים הם כנגד שבעים אומות שמתמעטים והולכים, סימן כליה היא להם.

The bulls of the festival are seventy in number, corresponding to the seventy nations that steadily decrease; this is a sign of destruction for them.

Considering the above two statements together would appear to present us with a contradiction regarding the seventy bulls and the seventy nations of the world:

- On the one hand, we see that the Gemara states that the seventy bulls are offered over Sukkos for the *benefit* of the seventy nations.
- On the other hand, the seventy bulls are offered in decreasing amounts over the course of the festival, denoting the progressive *decline* of those nations.

How can these two ideas be reconciled with each other?

The answer is that the ultimate blessing for the nations of the world is the diminishing of everything about them that is antithetical to Godly living. As long as they are fueled by the lust for temporal power and ascendancy, they will never be fully connected to Hashem's purpose in creating the world. Ultimately, the steady decline of everything that is unhealthy in these nations' worldview is the source of the greatest blessing they can attain.

What is most significant and thought-provoking here is that the festival of Sukkos, as we have noted numerous times, is dedicated to the unique and special relationship the Jewish People enjoy with Hashem. As such, one might well have expected the nations of the world to be entirely absent from our consciousness during these days, yet we see this is not the case. This tells us that having a fundamentally positive vision and wishes for the nations of the world is *part of* the unique mission of the Jewish People. The ultimate inclusion of the entire world in Hashem's plan is an integral part of the vision of the Jewish People themselves, as we express in our prayers on Rosh Hashanah and Yom Kippur: "ויעשו כולם אגודה אחת לעשות רצונך בלבב שלם—And they will all form one assembly to perform Your will with a full heart." Indeed, to this end, a primary role of the Jewish People is that of "a light unto the nations,"[4] spreading Hashem's message of how life should be lived to the entire world.

THE SEVENTY BULLS, PART II: AT HOME WITH THE ALMIGHTY

A very different explanation for the decreasing number of bulls offered over the course of Sukkos is found in the *Midrash Tanchuma*:

לימדה תורה דרך ארץ, שמי שיש לו אכסנאי, יום ראשון יאכילנו עופות, למחר יאכילנו דגים, למחר גבינה, למחר מאכילו קטנית, למחר ירק.

The Torah teaches us the proper conduct [lit., the way of the world], that if a person has a lodger, on the first day he feeds him fowl, the next day he feeds him fish, the next day cheese, on the next day he feeds him legumes, and on the next day vegetables.[5]

These words are quite striking. What does the way of the world (*derech eretz*) regarding the way one treats his guest have to do with the offerings in the Beis Hamikdash? Moreover, seemingly, the decreasing level of hospitality as the days go by may be part of human nature, but surely is not the ideal! Why then, should this be reflected in the way we

---

4   *Yeshayahu* 49:6.
5   *Parshas Pinchas*, sec. 17. See *Rashi* to *Bamidbar* loc. cit., verse 36, for a slightly different reading of the Midrash.

bring our offerings? Should we not be striving for the ideal, at least at this special time and in this special place?

The answer is that decreasing the level of hospitality *is* the ideal, for there is one thing the host can give the guest that is greater than hospitality, and that is to feel as if he is part of the household. After being in the home for a certain time, the guest doesn't want five-star treatment. He wants to be asked to help clear the table or wash the dishes! The idea of dwelling in the sukkah means moving in to Hashem's domain, so to speak. The decreasing number of *korbanos* thus represents the increasing level of feeling "at home" with Hashem. In this regard, the fewer the *korbanos*, the greater the connection.

This idea can be demonstrated from the halachah as well. *Hallel* is recited on every day of Sukkos and every day of Pesach. However, there is a difference between the two. On Pesach, the entire *Hallel* is recited only on the first day (in the Diaspora, the first two days); on the other days, half *Hallel* is said. By contrast, on Sukkos, we recite the whole *Hallel* every day. As mentioned above, the Gemara explains that the difference comes from the fact that Sukkos has different *korbanos* every day, thereby making each day like a separate Yom Tov, while Pesach has the same *korbanos* offered every day. Now, the amount of *korbanos* on each day of Sukkos differs on account of the fact that the number of bulls *decreases* each day, and yet the Gemara sees this as something special for each ensuing day! This underscores the idea that as the amount of *korbanos* decreases, the level of connection increases, making each day of Sukkos a greater Yom Tov than the day before![6]

Thus, an analysis of the *korbanos* of the festival, even though we are not currently bringing them, yields a fascinating perspective on the mitzvah of sukkah that we fulfill during these seven days.

TWO RAMS AND FOURTEEN LAMBS

In addition to the varying number of bulls that are offered over the course of the festival, the Torah also states that two rams and fourteen lambs should be offered each day. Although these numbers are constant,

---

6   R' Aharon Dovid Goldberg, *Shiras David, Moadim*, p. 156.

they too are revealing. We noted in an earlier chapter that Sukkos represents the culminating festival for two tracks of festivals in the Torah:

- It is the last of the *Shalosh Regalim*.
- It is the culmination of the *Yamim Noraim*.

The *mussaf* for every other festival involves one ram and seven lambs. As such, we note that the amount of these animals offered on Sukkos is double that of other festivals. This serves to emphasize the idea that, representing the conclusion of both sets of festivals, Sukkos is in fact two festivals rolled into one.

THE SACRIFICIAL ORDER:
BURNT OFFERINGS AND SIN OFFERINGS

On each day of the festival, in addition to the animals that are brought as *olah* (burnt) offerings, a goat is offered as a *chatas* (sin) offering. In this regard, the *mussaf* offerings of Sukkos are no different than those of every other festival. However, in one aspect, Sukkos is unique. The general rule is that whenever a group of *korbanos* includes both sin offerings and burnt offerings, the sin offerings are brought first.[7] This is notwithstanding the fact that the burnt offerings are normally mentioned first in the verse. The exception to the rule is the *mussaf* of Sukkos, where the Gemara derives from the relevant verses that the burnt offerings are brought first and the sin offering afterward.[8]

What lies behind this exceptional situation?

R' Leib Mintzberg explains that in order to understand the exception, we first need to understand the rule itself. The Gemara explains the reason the sin offering normally comes first through means of a parable.[9] If there is friction between two parties, one first needs to resolve that negative feeling before proceeding to present a gift. Likewise, a burnt offering is a gift; hence, one first needs to offer the sin offering

---

7   *Zevachim* 90a.
8   Ibid.
9   Ibid., 7b, cited by *Rashi* to *Vayikra* 5:8.

and thereby remove any negative element, and then he can proceed to bring the burnt offering.

Having explained the rule, we can now understand why Sukkos is different. Sukkos follows immediately after Yom Kippur, so our sins have just been cleared away. While it is true that we nevertheless bring a sin offering on Sukkos as well, this is because it is always possible that some sin has occurred in the meanwhile, which of course needs to be dealt with. However, the overwhelming atmosphere is one of celebration over having received atonement for the sins of the previous year. Hence, the urgency of the sin offering is deemphasized, for it does not constitute an impediment to the "gift" of the burnt offerings and can be offered after them.

On a deeper level, it is possible to see the sin offerings of Sukkos as continued atonement for the sins of the previous year, but from a different vantage point. Sometimes, if there is an impediment in a relationship, it needs to be repaired as a matter of priority, thereby allowing the relationship to get back on track. However, at that point, specifically after having experienced a renewed closeness, it is often appropriate to then apologize again. This apology is not critical to the restoring of the relationship; on the contrary, it is coming *from a place of* a restored relationship, in a way that can lead to even greater closeness. This is the sin offering of Sukkos. The sin offerings of Rosh Hashanah and Yom Kippur cleared the way to restore our relationship with Hashem, which we then celebrate on Sukkos. It is specifically from within the renewed relationship that we offer the sin offerings on Sukkos, to promote even further closeness. Accordingly, the unique nature of these sin offerings is demonstrated by the fact that they are brought after the burnt offerings.[10]

SE'IR AND SE'IR IZIM

As mentioned above, on each day of the festival, in addition to the animals that are brought as burnt offerings, a goat is offered as a *chatas*

---

10   Ben Melech, Sukkos, maamar 12.

offering. If we look closely at the verses for each day, we will notice that the way the Torah refers to this goat offering changes.

- On the first, second, and fourth days, it is called "*se'ir izim*."
- On the third, fifth, sixth, and seventh days, it is called simply "*se'ir*."

What is behind this shift in terminology?

We mentioned above that the seventy bulls offered on Sukkos correspond to the seventy nations of the world. In an earlier chapter, we cited the *Vilna Gaon* who says that these seventy nations are represented generally by the two nations of Yishmael and Eisav. In terms of our discussion, he cites the *Zohar*, which states that the term "*se'ir*" refers to Eisav, while the term "*se'ir izim*" refers to Yishmael. Accordingly:

- The *korbanos* offered on the first, second, and fourth days (thirteen, twelve, and ten, respectively) total thirty-five. Hence the term "*se'ir izim*" is used on those days, referring to Yishmael, who represents those thirty-five nations.
- The *korbanos* offered on the other four days (eleven, nine, eight, and seven) likewise total thirty-five, and on those days the term "*se'ir*" is used, referring to Eisav, who represents those nations.[11]

In the *Mussaf* prayer, we ask for the rebuilding of the Beis Hamikdash and the restoration of the offering of *korbanos*. In the meanwhile, we remember them in our prayers and in the Torah reading. In this regard, the insights we receive into these *korbanos* allow them to continue to speak to us. The more we absorb and implement their messages, the more we are able to achieve, in some measure, the basic goal of a *korban*, which comes from the word "*karov*," meaning "near"—drawing nearer to Hashem in our own lives through enhanced vision and elevated deeds.

---

11   *Kol Eliyahu, Parshas Pinchas.*

CHAPTER 17

NISUCH HAMAYIM AND SIMCHAS BEIS HASHOEIVAH

PART I: NISUCH HAMAYIM

One of the unique *korbanos* of Sukkos is the *nisuch hamayim*—water libation. Every day of the year, wine is poured out on the *Mizbeiach*. On the seven days of Sukkos, the Torah mandates that water also be poured out alongside the wine.

What is the significance of offering water on the *Mizbeiach* during Sukkos? The Gemara itself addresses this question and explains that since on Sukkos we are judged regarding water, we bring an offering of water in order to be judged favorably.[1]

WHEN WATERS CRY

A fascinating additional element within the water libation as it relates to Sukkos is found in the *Shem MiShmuel*. He refers to a Midrash that discusses the background to *nisuch hamayim*, tracing it back to the second day of Creation, when Hashem divided between the higher and lower waters. The Midrash relates that the lowers waters were crying

---

1   *Rosh Hashanah* 16a.

at being distanced from Hashem. In response, Hashem promised them that they would be offered on the *Mizbeiach* every year during the festival of Sukkos. Additionally, salt, which comes from seawater, would be offered alongside each and every *korban* on a daily basis throughout the year.[2]

As we have seen, a prominent part of the festivities during Sukkos is in celebration of having received atonement from Hashem during Rosh Hashanah and Yom Kippur. Indeed, the Gemara records that many of the songs that were sung during those festivities were focused on the theme of *teshuvah*. Sukkos is thus the festival of *kiruv rechokim*—bringing close that which was distant. In keeping with this theme of *kiruv rechokim*, the centerpiece of the celebration is water, which was the first entity to be distanced from Hashem and is now being brought close once again, embodying this idea on a most elemental level.

SUKKOS AND AHARON

The *Shem MiShmuel* adds that this idea will further highlight the connection between Sukkos and the personality of Aharon. The basic connection can be seen through the idea of the *Ananei Hakavod*, which are commemorated on Sukkos and which the Gemara informs us came through the merit of Aharon. One of the primary endeavors with which Aharon is associated is that of *kiruv rechokim*. In *Pirkei Avos*, Hillel exhorts us to be like the students of Aharon, among whose pursuits he lists, "אוהב את הבריות ומקרבן לתורה—One who loves people and brings them close to Torah."[3] As such, the message and personality of Aharon run through Sukkos, the festival that celebrates the bringing close of that which was distant.

INSIDE WATER

It is possible to take this discussion one stage deeper. The basis of receiving atonement on Yom Kippur is the fact that the Jew has an inner essence that cannot be corrupted or sullied. It is from this inner

---

2   *Bereishis Rabbah* 5:3.

3   1:12.

essence that he builds out, disassociating himself from any misdeeds as not being reflective of his true essence, but rather of external circumstance. The Hebrew term for atonement, *kapparah*, actually means "to wipe away."[4] The *avodah* of Yom Kippur is for the person to identify with his inner core and present his sins as extrinsic to his being, and which can thus be wiped away. Paralleling this, we find that on Yom Kippur, the Kohen Gadol is able to enter the Holy of Holies, which is known as *"lifnai velifnim*—inside the inside,"[5] to perform the Divine service there. When he enters that place, he enables the people to also access their own innermost place, thereby achieving atonement. To put it slightly differently, what enables a person to draw close after being distant is the fact that there is a part of him that remained close the entire time.

It is fascinating to see this idea, too, reflected in the coming close of the water. As we have seen, one of the two consolations Hashem offered the water, in addition to being brought on the *Mizbeiach* as water on Sukkos, was that it would also be brought in the form of salt every day. The salt that exists within water cannot readily be seen just by looking at the water, but it resides within there just the same. As such, like atonement itself, the water is able to reconnect when the time comes because there is an inner aspect of it that was connected the entire time.

Very beautiful!

PART II: SIMCHAS BEIS HASHOEIVAH

Sukkos is referred to in the prayers as *"zman simchaseinu*—the time of our joy," and nowhere was this joy felt and expressed more than in the Beis Hamikdash, where special celebrations were held on each night of the festival. And indeed, this is most fitting, for Sukkos celebrates the special relationship the Jewish People have with the Divine Presence. As such, the Beis Hamikdash, where the Divine Presence resides, forms the natural setting for celebrating that relationship.

---

4   See *Rashi* to *Bereishis* 32:21, s.v. *"achaprah."*
5   See *Horayos* 13a.

As we have discussed, on each day of Sukkos, water was poured out on the *Mizbeiach*. Each night, the drawing of the water from a nearby spring was accompanied by special festivities, in keeping with the verse, "וּשְׁאַבְתֶּם מַיִם בְּשָׂשׂוֹן מִמַּעַיְנֵי הַיְשׁוּעָה"—You shall draw forth water with joy, from the wellsprings of salvation."[6] Indeed, the celebration on the nights of Sukkos was so great that the Sages remarked, "Whoever did not see the joy of the drawing of the water, never saw joy in his days."[7]

Simchah and Sasson

Two words for joy that feature recurrently in the festival of Sukkos are "*sasson*" and "*simchah*." There is no such thing as a synonym in *lashon hakodesh*, so when two words denote a similar idea, each embodies a distinctive aspect of that idea.

What is the specific difference between *sasson* and *simchah*?

R' Yitzchak Maltzen explains that *simchah* reflects joy that is felt, but not necessarily expressed in action, while *sasson* denotes joy that finds physical expression and celebration.[8] Thus, for example, we introduce the middle section of the Yom Tov *Amidah* by saying:

וַתִּתֶּן לָנוּ ה' אֱלֹקֵינוּ בְּאַהֲבָה מוֹעֲדִים לְשִׂמְחָה חַגִּים וּזְמַנִּים לְשָׂשׂוֹן.

You gave us, Hashem our God, appointed times for simchah, festivals and special times for sasson.

- The term "*Moadim*" encompasses all the special days in the Jewish year, both the *Shalosh Regalim* as well as the *Yamim Noraim*. All of these are days of *simchah*, for even the *Yamim Noraim* are accompanied by a feeling of joy at the prospect of being judged with benevolence and receiving atonement, thereby being cleansed from our sins. However, due to the solemn nature of those days, they are not accompanied by outward celebration; hence, the *Moadim* as a whole are characterized by the term "*simchah*."

---

6   *Yeshayahu* 12:3.

7   *Sukkah* 51a.

8   Commentary *Siach Yitzchak* in *Siddur Ishei Yisrael, Shalosh Regalim*.

- The "festivals and special times" refer specifically to the *Shalosh Regalim*. On these days, our joy can be outwardly expressed, and thus we associate them with "*sasson*."

Hence, when the verse says to "draw forth water with *sasson*," it is indicating that the drawing of the water should be accompanied not only with a feeling of joy, but with actual celebration.

Here we must ask the most basic of questions: Why should the drawing of water be a cause for such celebration—or any celebration, for that matter? It is true that this water will be used for a mitzvah, but we do not find such celebration accompanying any other mitzvos or their preparations? Moreover, to further accentuate the question, we know that on Rosh Hashanah and Yom Kippur we do not say *Hallel*, even though they are also *Yamim Tovim*. The Gemara explains that since these are days of judgment, the recitation of the festive song of *Hallel* is not appropriate for such a time.[9] Sukkos, too, is a time when we are judged regarding water for the coming year; yet the drawing of water is accompanied by a celebration the likes of which outshines any other of the entire year!

R' Dovid Cohen explains that the reason the drawing of the water is the cause for such celebration is because of the message it contains for everyone present about their own existence.[10] As we have seen, the water was originally distanced from the higher realms, where it was before Hashem, to the lower realms of the physical world. On Sukkos, Hashem demonstrates that even something that is distant from Him can draw near through being used for Divine service. This idea casts the totality of physical existence in a different light. The physical world—distant from Hashem as it seems to be—is now full of opportunity. Water, one of the simplest and most basic physical entities, can be raised up from the depths, and so can the world and those who live in it—and that is true cause for celebration!

---

9   *Arachin* 11a.
10   *Zman Simchaseinu*, chap. 36.

The Mishnah in the fifth chapter of *Maseches Sukkah* details the various aspects of the *Beis Hashoeivah* celebrations. It states that the procession would begin in the courtyard of the Beis Hamikdash, from where they would descend the fifteen steps that lead out from the courtyard, which parallel the fifteen chapters in *Tehillim* that begin "*Shir Hamaalos*—A song of elevations." As part of the procession, they would sound the shofar while at the top of the steps, again when they reached the tenth step, and once more when they descended all the steps.

What is the relevance of the fifteen steps in the Beis Hamikdash to the *Beis Hashoeivah* celebrations? Additionally, Why did they stop to sound the shofar at the tenth step, which is neither the top nor the bottom of the steps? Perhaps more fundamentally, What is the significance of the fifteen steps in the first place?

The *Maharal* explains that the fifteen steps, which are called *maalos*, represent the fifteen levels of elevation a person can achieve in this world.[11] The number fifteen corresponds to the two letters *yud* and *hei*, which make up the Divine name "י-ה," and whose numerical value is fifteen. The Gemara states that with these two letters, Hashem created two worlds: this world with the letter *hei* and the World to Come with the letter *yud*.[12] The fusion of the two letters indicates the possibility of achieving and experiencing all fifteen levels—even an element of those that belong to the World to Come—in this world.

In truth, this concept has already been experienced by the Jewish People in their most formative period. In the Haggadah, we mention the many kindnesses that Hashem bestowed upon our ancestors from when they left Egypt until they entered the Land of Israel and built the Beis Hamikdash, saying that each one would have enough (*dayeinu*) to thank Hashem for. Interestingly, the number of things we mention is fifteen. More interestingly, we do not refer to them as "חסדים—kindnesses," but as "מעלות—elevations." The point is that we thank Hashem for giving us these experiences that allowed us to ascend

---

11   *Gevuros Hashem*, chap. 59.
12   *Menachos* 29b.

fifteen levels, culminating in the building of the Beis Hamikdash, the place in this world where it is possible to come closest to the Divine.

As we have seen, the focal point of the joy surrounding the *Beis Hashoeivah* is the recognition that even the most mundane things of this world can be connected to Hashem—from within this world. As such, the fusion of the two worlds represented by the fifteen steps is of utmost relevance as we begin those celebrations. We now also understand why the shofar was blown, not only at the top and the bottom of the steps, but also at the tenth step, indicating that the fifteen steps actually comprise two distinct realms—represented by the numbers ten and five—which are being unified and combined.[13]

FROM THE BEIS HASHOEIVAH–BEING THERE

The Gemara relates that when Hillel would rejoice during the *Beis Hashoeivah* celebrations, he would say:

אם אני כאן הכל כאן. ואם אין אני כאן, מי כאן?

If I am here, then everything is here. And if I am not here, then who is here?

This is a rather puzzling statement, especially coming from Hillel, who was known as an extremely humble and forbearing person. What was his intent with these words, and what lesson did he wish to impart?

The *Netziv* explains Hillel's statement as follows:[14] The *Beis Hashoeivah* celebrations in the Beis Hamikdash presented the people with a rare opportunity to connect fully with the Divine Presence in His abode. Indeed, the *Talmud Yerushalmi* explains that the reason this event was known as "*Beis Hashoeivah*—the House of Drawing Forth" is because it was possible to draw forth *ruach hakodesh* (Divine

---

13   This will add further illumination to the Mishnah's description there that as they were leaving the Beis Hamikdash premises to draw the water, they would declare, "Our ancestors degraded and abandoned the Beis Hamikdash, however, as for us, "אנו לי-ה"—we belong only to God." The choice of the Divine name "ה-י" in that setting reflects the intent to attain the fifteen levels of elevation reflected by that name, the fifteenth and highest of which is made attainable by the Beis Hamikdash.

14   *Harchev Davar* to *Shemos* 5:3.

inspiration) through the spiritual heights that were reached during the celebrations.[15] Regarding this, Hillel added one stipulation: the person needs to be there—totally. It is possible to participate in an event without being fully present. One may turn up and go through all the motions, but his thoughts are not focused on where he is and he is not emotionally engaged in what is happening.

The word "כל" is a term that is used to represent the Divine Presence.[16] What Hillel was doing was reminding himself and others that "if I am here, i.e., fully and in every sense of the word, then the 'Everything' i.e., Hashem, will be here to meet me. However, if I am not here in any real sense, then who is here?" I cannot expect to encounter the Divine Presence when I myself am not present.

We currently do not have the *Beis Hashoeivah*. However, Hillel's message bears remembering for all the encounters we do have with elevated moments and events. There is much there waiting for us when we arrive; we just need to be sure to be there when we do.

---

15   *Sukkah* 5:1.
16   See *Ramban* to *Bereishis* 24:1.

THE CONCLUDING DAYS OF SUKKOS

CHAPTER 18

HOSHANA RABBAH

INTRODUCTION: DAY SEVEN–AND DAY TWO

From a halachic standpoint, the status of the seventh day of Sukkos, known as Hoshana Rabbah, is identical to that of the other intermediate days of the festival. However, there are various customs that apply to this day that would appear to ascribe to it a higher status than the rest. For example, the additional chapters of *Tehillim* recited in *Pesukei D'Zimrah* on Shabbos and Yom Tov are recited on this day as well, additional candles are lit in shul as on Yom Kippur, and the chazzan wears a *kittel* as on Yom Kippur.

Indeed, the special nature of the seventh day of Sukkos is identified in the Talmud itself. The verse in *Yeshayahu* reads: "ואותי יום יום ידרשון."[1] The simple explanation of the double phrase "יום יום" is "every day," so that the verse means "They seek Me [Hashem] out every day." However, the *Yerushalmi* explains the phrase "יום יום" as referring to two particular days in the year that are auspicious for seeking out Hashem in prayer: Rosh Hashanah and Hoshana Rabbah.[2]

---

1   58:2.
2   *Yerushalmi, Rosh Hashanah* 4:8.

What is the special nature of Hoshana Rabbah, and by virtue of what does it constitute the second of the "two days of prayer," alongside Rosh Hashanah?

PART I: SUKKOS, HOSHANA RABBAH, AND WATER

The *Tur* and *Shulchan Aruch*[3] explain that the background to these special customs lies in the Mishnah that informs us that on Sukkos we are judged concerning the rainfall for the coming year.[4] This judgment takes place over the entire seven days of Sukkos. Indeed, according to the Gemara, it has an integral role in the mitzvos we perform during the festival:

- *Nisuch hamayim*: The Gemara states, "Said the Holy One, blessed is He, bring before Me water libations on the *Mizbeiach* on Sukkos, so that the rainfall for the [coming] year will be blessed for you."[5]
- *Arba minim*: Elsewhere, the Gemara states that the *arba minim*, all of which require an abundance of water in order to grow, are taken on Sukkos as a means to elicit favor regarding water for the coming year.[6]

The implications of this idea are that the position of Sukkos within the agricultural year has twofold significance, one facing backward and one facing forward:

- On the one hand, it celebrates the gathering of the harvest of the previous year.
- On the other hand, it is a time when we are judged concerning the water supply for the year ahead.

---

3   *Orach Chaim* 660.
4   *Rosh Hashanah* 1:2.
5   *Rosh Hashanah* 16b.
6   *Taanis* 2b.

CLOSING AND BEGINNING

In truth, it is possible to see these two elements within the verses describing Sukkos.

- In *Parshas Mishpatim*: Sukkos is referred to as "חג האסיף בצאת השנה באספך את מעשיך מן השדה—The festival of ingathering at the **close of** the year, when you bring in your work from the field."[7] This verse focuses entirely on the harvest that has been brought in that year, which is now coming to a close.
- In *Parshas Ki Sisa*: Sukkos is referred to as "חג האסיף תקופת השנה—The festival of the ingathering, at the **changing of** the year."[8] *Rashi* explains this latter phrase to denote the fact that a new year is beginning. In this verse, the focus is thus also on the year ahead.

CELEBRATION AND ADJUDICATION

On the face of it, the celebration over the ingathering of the harvest and the judgment concerning rainfall appear incongruous with each other; after all, when one is being judged it is not a time for celebration! However, upon further reflection, it is possible to see how the celebration actually aids in the judgment. In *Parshas Emor*, the Torah commands regarding Sukkos, "באספכם את תבואת הארץ תחוגו את חג ה' שבעת ימים—When you gather in the produce of the land, you shall celebrate Hashem's festival for seven days." Sukkos is referred to as "Hashem's festival," since the purpose of the celebration is recognizing that the harvest from that year came from Hashem's blessing. In this regard, we may say that this celebration itself and the recognition it entails will augur well for the Jewish People to be deserving of further blessing from Hashem in the rainfall of the year ahead!

THE SEVENTH DAY

And yet, as much as the judgment occurs throughout all seven days of the festival, critical emphasis is laid on the seventh day, since it is the

---

7   *Shemos* 23:16.
8   Ibid., 34:22.

final day and thus, the most decisive. This, therefore, is the background to the extra prayers that are added on Hoshana Rabbah, as well as the other customs mentioned in the *Tur* and *Shulchan Aruch*, expressing the significance of this final day.

PART II: ROSH HASHANAH, YOM KIPPUR, AND HOSHANA RABBAH

An additional element within the day of Hoshana Rabbah is found in the *Zohar*.[9] Although a person's judgment for the year is inscribed on Rosh Hashanah and sealed on Yom Kippur, the scrolls containing the judgment, representing its implementation, only "go out" on Hoshana Rabbah. As such, this day represents the opportunity to recall those scrolls and perhaps to replace them with more favorable ones.[10] Therefore, the prayers and atmosphere on Hoshana Rabbah are akin to those of Yom Kippur, with the same goal in mind.

Here, too, we note the seeming incongruity of the two themes of seriousness and celebration. After all, Hoshana Rabbah is the seventh day of Sukkos and, as such, it is still part of the Festival of our Joy. How does this go together with the idea that it is the final Day of Judgment and atonement?

And yet, in terms of the *Zohar*'s description, the actual judgment has already been completed on Yom Kippur; all that remains is for the scrolls containing that judgment to be delivered. At this stage, perhaps the greatest thing that one who is in need of a recalling of his scroll can do is to perform the mitzvos with joy! Maybe this merit itself will serve to mitigate against any negative judgment he received and grant him clemency. And so, on this unique and special day, the melodies of *Hallel* and those of the *Yamim Noraim* intermingle, and supplications for forgiveness are offered within just a few minutes of having waved the

---

9   *Parshas Tzav* 31b.
10   This is the basis of the traditional greeting on Hoshana Rabbah, where people wish each other *"piska tava"* in Aramaic, or *"a gutten kvittel"* in Yiddish, which means, "a good note."

arba minim in jubilation. For at times such as this, in addition to prayer from the heart, the "best defense" is a mitzvah performed with joy!

THE SECOND SEAL

However, the significance of Hoshana Rabbah goes beyond the idea of a final chance for repeal for someone who has, Heaven forbid, received a negative judgment; it is an important day for those who received a positive judgment as well. Hoshana Rabbah is referred to in the early sources as "*Yom Hachosam*—the Day of the Seal."[11] Apparently, this means that the judgment a person received during the *Yamim Noraim* is sealed on this day. However, this naturally begs the question: Is our judgment for the year not sealed on Yom Kippur, as we say, "On Rosh Hashanah they shall be written and on the day of the Yom Kippur they shall be sealed?" The *Arizal* explains that the seal of Hoshana Rabbah is in addition to that of Yom Kippur.[12] Why do we need two seals? The halachah states that when it comes to particularly sensitive matters, one seal is not considered sufficient, as there is the chance that it may be tampered with. However, a double seal is considered to be beyond concern for mishap.[13] Similarly, the seal we receive on Yom Kippur carries the risk of being "tampered with" by forces of evil during the course of the year. To this end, on Hoshana Rabbah, through heartfelt prayer and repentance with joy, we seek to secure a second seal to vouchsafe our positive judgment from any mishap.[14]

PART III: TAKING THE ARAVAH

Among the unique customs of Hoshana Rabbah—indeed, the oldest of its customs, dating back to the times of the prophets[15]—is the taking of the *aravah* (willow) branch. In the Beis Hamikdash, aside from the *aravah* that is part of the *arba minim*, there is an additional

---

11 See Rabbeinu Bachya, *Kad Hakemach*, s.v. "*aravah.*"
12 *Pri Eitz Chaim* 29:4.
13 See *Avodah Zarah* 29b.
14 *Bnei Yissaschar, Tishrei, maamar* 12.
15 See *Sukkah* 44a.

Torah-mandated mitzvah to take an *aravah* branch. The Gemara states that this mitzvah is in the category known as "*halachah l'Moshe miSinai*—an oral law transmitted from Hashem to Moshe at Sinai."[16] In the Beis Hamikdash itself, the mitzvah of *aravah* applies on all seven days of Sukkos. However, the custom of taking the *aravah* outside of the Mikdash is only on the seventh day.[17] Opinions differ as to whether this custom involves waving the *aravah* branch or beating it against something.[18] Our custom, therefore, is to do both.

BEATING THE PROSECUTION

The Gemara relates that part of the custom of taking the *aravah* on Hoshana Rabbah is beating it on the ground. One of the Geonim, Rav Tzemach Gaon,[19] explains the background to this practice, based on the Midrash that relates each of the *arba minim* to a different part of the body:[20]

- The *esrog* corresponds to the heart.
- The *lulav* corresponds to the spine.
- The *hadasim* correspond to the eyes.
- The *aravos* correspond to the lips.

Rav Tzemach explains that on this auspicious and sensitive day of Hoshana Rabbah, we undertake to improve the speech that comes from our lips. Thus, we beat the *aravah*, which corresponds to the lips, on the ground as a declaration of intent to stamp out and eradicate harmful and negative forms of speech.

Rav Tzemach then offers a second explanation for this custom. There is a concept known as *mekatregim*, accusers. R' Moshe Chaim Luzzatto explains that the concept of accusers is a great kindness from Hashem, whereby even if a person has sinned, he is not punished unless the

---

16   *Sukkah* ibid.
17   Although strictly speaking, one *aravah* branch suffices to fulfill one's obligation, the wide-spread custom, based on the *Arizal*, is to take five branches (see *Mishnah Berurah* 664:16).
18   See *Rashi, Sukkah* 44b, s.v. "*chavit*," and *Rambam, Hilchos Lulav* 7:22.
19   *Teshuvos HaGeonim, Shaarei Teshuvah* 340.
20   *Vayikra Rabbah* 30:14.

additional step has been taken of having an accusation made against him from on high.[21] It is with reference to these accusers that we ask in the *Avinu Malkeinu* prayer: "סתום פיות משטינינו ומקטריגנו—Seal the mouths of our adversaries and accusers." In this vein, Rav Tzemach explains that we beat the *aravah* on the ground in order to silence the mouths of our accusers on high.

It is very meaningful to consider that these two explanations for beating the *aravah* are not as distinct from one another as they might seem, for the one follows from the other. What determines whether an accusation will, in fact, be made? The answer, says the Chafetz Chaim, is whether the person himself levels accusations against others.[22] This is a very striking application of the idea of *middah keneged middah*, measure for measure: If a person accuses others, exposing and announcing their faults and shortcomings, then he is dealt with accordingly, and his own misdeeds are announced by accusers in the Heavenly Court.

Accordingly, when we beat the *aravah* on the ground in order to silence our accusers, we also undertake with sincerity to desist from harmful speech, for it is in the merit of the latter that the former can be achieved!

---

21   *Derech Hashem*, sec. 2, chap. 6.
22   *Shemiras Halashon, Shaar Hazechirah*, chap. 2.

CHAPTER 19

SHEMINI ATZERES AND SIMCHAS TORAH

THE NATURE AND GOAL OF THE FINAL DAY

Immediately following the seven days of Sukkos is a final day of Yom Tov—Shemini Atzeres. In contrast to the week of Sukkos, this Yom Tov has no specific mitzvos attached to it; it is simply a Yom Tov. Even the name given to it by the Torah, *Atzeres*, derives from the word "לעצור," meaning "to stop." This seems to further indicate that the primary element of this day is purely that we "stop," i.e., refrain from performing *melachah* (productive labor).

What is the unique role and nature of Shemini Atzeres?

Rashi, in his commentary in *Parshas Emor*, explains the background to this final day as follows:

> [The matter can be compared] to a king who invited his sons
> for a number of days. When the time came for them to part, he
> said, "Please, my sons, stay with me one more day, it is difficult
> for me to part from you."[1]

---

1   *Vayikra* 23:36.

On the face of it, it is difficult to understand how staying one more day will resolve the difficulty in parting; surely, it will only delay that occurrence! Indeed, if anything, staying another day will only make it more difficult to part when the time comes, since every day brings them closer together.

In addition to being Yom Tov, the Sages also chose Shemini Atzeres as the day on which we conclude the yearly Torah-reading cycle and begin next year's cycle.[2] Many commentators raise the question as to why this day was chosen as the time to conclude and restart the year's Torah reading. Is this not something that would be more appropriate to do on Rosh Hashanah, the beginning of the new year?

THE MEANING OF THE WORD "ATZERES"

R' Azariah Fego explains that the word "atzeres" does not only mean "to stop," it also means "to contain."[3] The month of Tishrei is filled with immensely powerful days—Rosh Hashanah, Yom Kippur, and Sukkos—each one replete with its messages, experiences, reflections, and realizations. These days usher in the new year, and indeed they are meant to serve as the launch for the year, with their attainments and insights accompanying us during the months ahead. For that reason, it is critically important that this festive season end with a day of Atzeres, a day dedicated to containing and retaining all that we have achieved. This way, all of our attainments over the Yamim Noraim and Sukkos will not be left behind in the month of Tishrei. And so, there are no further distinctive mitzvos on this day; there is no shofar, sukkah, or arba minim. All we need to "do" is stop, retain, absorb, and integrate before setting out into the year ahead.

This is the meaning of the Midrash cited by Rashi regarding the role of the final day. After being together with Hashem for seven days, it is difficult for Him to part from us. The solution to this problem is the final day. If we use it properly to maintain the connection that we forged and

---

2   In Eretz Yisrael, this takes place on Shemini Atzeres itself. In the Diaspora, it takes place on the second day of this final Yom Tov, which is thus called Simchas Torah.

3   Drashos Binah L'Ittim, drush 17.

renewed during Sukkos, then there will be *no need* to separate afterward, for even as the festival of Sukkos will have concluded, the relationship will remain with us and accompany us throughout the year.

STAYING IN TOUCH

This brings us to Simchas Torah. Shemini Atzeres represents the crucial importance of staying in touch with the experiences of the *Yamim Noraim* throughout the year, so much so that the Torah set aside a final day of Yom Tov purely for this purpose. Taking their cue from this, the Sages added something that will be of further help to us in this regard. They instituted this final Yom Tov as the point in the year where we conclude the Torah-reading cycle and begin a new one. Launching the Torah reading on this day initiates a program that will allow us to remain connected to these days throughout the course of the year. In order to understand how this might be, let us go back to the roots of the original enactment of reading from the Torah.

The Gemara provides the background to the reading of the Torah in public on Mondays, Thursdays, and Shabbos, indicating that this enactment goes back to the earliest days of the Jewish People in the desert:

> *"And they traveled three days in the desert and they did not find water."*[4] *Those who expound verses metaphorically said "water" refers to Torah, as it says: "Ho, all who are thirsty go to the water."*[5] *As soon as they went three days without "water," they instantly became weary [and complained]. The prophets among them arose and instituted that they should read from the Torah on Shabbos, Monday, and Thursday, in order that they not go three days without Torah.*[6]

It is interesting to consider when exactly were these three days—empty of Torah learning—that led us to act contentiously. How far into our wanderings in the desert were we? The Gemara doesn't discuss it.

---

4   *Shemos* 15:22.
5   *Yeshayahu* 55:1.
6   *Bava Kama* 82a.

However, if we look at the verses in their source, we will see that these were the three days *immediately following* the passing of the Jewish People through the Red Sea.

This casts everything the Gemara says in an entirely new light.

The splitting of the Red Sea was one of the greatest miracles ever experienced by our people. One can only imagine the feelings of euphoria, elevation, and inspiration that we felt as we passed through the sea with the water as walls on either side. Emerging on the other side, we saw that our oppressors of so many decades who had chased after us to capture and re-enslave us had been drowned, and we were finally free. The feelings of inspiration from that occasion would no doubt stay with us for months—if not years—to come!

In the event, the Gemara says they lasted for three days.

The crucial lesson here is that as uplifting as any experience may be, that elevation is in danger of dissipating fairly swiftly if a person does not take steps to preserve it. Returning to one's everyday concerns can serve to dull very quickly the inspiration felt just a couple of days earlier.

Equally crucial to note is the measure that was introduced as the antidote to this dissipation—the institution of regular Torah learning. How does learning Torah achieve this aim?

An elevating event comes from a place of elevated living. It is an experience that calls a person to rise above his mundane concerns and lead a meaningful and idealistic existence. Once a person reengages in his day-to-day affairs, he loses his connection with that message; he ceases "speaking that language," and hence the effects of that inspiring event are liable to become lost.

The study of Torah serves to keep a person connected to the elevated place where that event came from. It serves to maintain a consciousness that higher (and Godlier) things are expected of him. Moreover, it does not make any difference which area of Torah one may be studying, for the underlying theme of all Torah study is determining how Hashem wants one to act in any given situation, how He wants the world to look, and what one can do to help make it look that way. That awareness keeps a person "logged in" to the source and substance of his elevating experiences.

In the same vein, the Sages judged that an invaluable way to retain our consciousness and sensitivity to the themes, concepts, and values that we connected with so strongly during the *Yamim Noraim* is to maintain an ongoing involvement in Torah learning.

This is what is represented by beginning the yearly reading cycle on Shemini Atzeres. The goal is that as far as we go into the year ahead, those days and weeks will be impacted and elevated by all that we encountered and acquired during the *Yamim Noraim* and Sukkos.

SEVEN PLUS SEVEN–TORAH REVERSE ENGINEERING

The idea of preserving and protecting the concepts with which we connected over the festivals of Tishrei is also reflected in the custom of *hakafos*, circling the *bimah* seven times, which we do on Simchas Torah. In an earlier chapter we noted, based on the *Yerushalmi*, that the practice of circling the *bimah* once on each of day of Sukkos and then seven times on the seventh day parallels the events of the conquest of Jericho, where these circuits led to the toppling of the walls of the city. Likewise, on Sukkos, we are looking to breach and topple the walls that separate between us and Hashem. However, this begs the question: If the walls that obstruct between us and Hashem have already been toppled by the seven circuits on Hoshana Rabbah, What further purpose is served by having another seven circuits on Simchas Torah? Are we looking to topple them again?

The *Shem MiShmuel* explains that the goal of the seven *hakafos* of Simchas Torah is not to *destroy* walls, but to *create* them. Having toppled the walls of impurity that separate between us and the Torah during Sukkos, we then proceed to take the Torah scroll and use it to circuit another seven times around the *bimah* on Simchas Torah, thereby creating walls of sanctity. For the Torah provides us with protection against the forces that would seek to rob us of the spiritual levels and sensitivities we attained during the elevated days of Rosh Hashanah, Yom Kippur, and Sukkos. By using the Torah to build a wall around those attainments, we look forward to having them accompany us throughout the year—informing, illuminating, and elevating all that we do.

CHAPTER 20

SHEMINI ATZERES
AND THE JEWISH PEOPLE

INTRODUCTION: A SEPARATE FESTIVAL?

There is a certain duality that marks the festival of Shemini Atzeres. On the one hand, as its name suggests, it is the eighth and final day of Sukkos, while on the other, it is also a self-contained festival. Thus, for example, in contrast to the last day of Pesach, we recite the *Shehecheyanu* blessing in *Kiddush* on Shemini Atzeres, indicating that we have reached a new festival.[1]

What lies behind this dual status?

THE FEAST ON THE FINAL DAY

The Gemara notes that in marked contrast to the seventy bulls that are offered in the Beis Hamikdash over the course of the festival of Sukkos, Shemini Atzeres is accompanied by only one bull.[2] The Gemara explains that while the seventy bulls of Sukkos correspond to the seventy nations of the world, the one bull of Shemini Atzeres corresponds to the Jewish People themselves. The Gemara then adds a parable:

---

1   See *Sukkah* 48a for other aspects whereby Shemini Atzeres is considered a distinct festival.
2   *Sukkah* 55b.

149

משל למלך בשר ודם שאמר לעבדיו עשו לי סעודה גדולה, ליום אחרון אמר
לאוהבו עשה לי סעודה קטנה כדי שאהנה ממך.

This can be compared to an earthly king who said to his servants, "Make for me a grand feast." On the final day, he said to his beloved, "Make for me a modest feast so that I may enjoy your company."

We see from here that while for the duration of Sukkos, the emphasis is on Israel as Hashem's people in the inclusionary sense of spreading His message to the entire world, including bringing offerings on their behalf, Shemini Atzeres is entirely devoted to the exclusive relationship between Israel and Hashem. As such, while it is a progression of the general theme of Sukkos, it has a nature and character all to its own.

THE TORAH READING FOR SIMCHAS TORAH

Indeed, the *Meshech Chochmah* explains that this is what lies behind the reading of *Parshas Vezos Haberachah* on Simchas Torah.[3] This is not just a matter of fortuitous timing to coincide with the end of the Torah-reading cycle; after all, the Torah reading on a festival needs to reflect an essential theme of that festival. Rather, the verses in *Vezos Haberachah* describe how Hashem chose the Jewish People from among the nations to give them His Torah as a heritage.[4] The reading continues in this vein, highlighting the special relationship between Hashem and the Jewish People, and concludes Moshe's blessing to the people with the words, "אין כא-ל ישורון...אשריך ישראל מי כמוך—There is none like the God of Yeshurun...Fortunate are you, O Israel, who is like you?" The Midrash on that verse amplifies this idea:

ישראל אומרים "אין כא-ל," ורוח הקודש אומרת "אשריך ישראל מי כמוך."

Israel says, "There is none like God," and the Divine spirit says, "Fortunate are you, O Israel, who is like you?"[5]

---

3   End of *Parshas Vezos Haberachah.*
4   *Devarim* 33:2–4.
5   *Sifri*, sec. 355.

These sentiments, expressing Hashem's love for His people, are indeed most appropriate as the Torah reading on Shemini Atzeres, the festival that celebrates that love and the special connection that emanates from it.

SHEMINI ATZERES AND PRAYER

The special nature of the festival of Shemini Atzeres not only bestows upon it a unique atmosphere, but also makes it a day of unique opportunity. The *Zohar* writes concerning this day:

> On the day of Shemini Atzeres, the Jewish People are invited to delight with the King, blessed be He, to receive from Him blessings for the days of the coming year. At that time of joy, there is no one with the King except for Israel. And one who sits before the King, and whom the King takes to sit before Him, he can ask whatever he desires and it will be given to him from the King's house.[6]

Shemini Atzeres is a particularly auspicious day for prayer. This is especially important to take note of, since we may have not intuitively associated prayer with this day in such a significant way; perhaps we would have ascribed prayer more to the earlier days of Tishrei, and celebration to these later days. To this end, the *Zohar* informs us that it is specifically the intimate and exclusive nature of the celebration on this final day that makes it so propitious for prayers and requests. Let us therefore take note of these words of the *Zohar* and make optimum use of the opportunity of this day to pour our hearts out in prayer before the King. And may we all be blessed with a year of happiness, fulfillment, and success in every sphere!

---

6   3:32a.

CHAPTER 21

TEFILLAS GESHEM

A highlight in the prayers on Shemini Atzeres is *Tefillas Geshem*, the Prayer for Rain. In this prayer, we mention our patriarchs' and forebears' various associations with water and ask Hashem to bless the year's rainfall in their merit.[1] Some of the episodes we recall and expressions we employ during this prayer seem quite striking at first. However, further contemplation through the medium of the commentators serves to shed additional light on those episodes and ideas themselves.

MOSHE'S MESIRUS NEFESH AT THE ROCK

זכור משוי בתיבת גמא מן המים...סגוליך עת צמאו למים על הסלע הך ויצאו מים, בצדקו חון חשרת מים.

Remember the one [Moshe] drawn forth in a basket of reeds from the water...at the time Your treasure [the Children of Israel] thirsted for water, he struck the rock and out came water—for the sake of his righteousness, grant abundant water![2]

---

1   In the Land of Israel, the custom is to recite this prayer before the congregation says the silent *Amidah* of *Mussaf*. In the Diaspora, it is recited in the chazzan's repetition of *Mussaf*.

2   *Tefillas Geshem*.

Many commentators express wonder at this section of the prayer. As we know, in the episode to which it refers, known as *Mei Merivah*, Hashem specifically told Moshe to speak to the rock, and his decision to hit it instead was considered a grave sin on his part for which he paid dearly, forfeiting the privilege of entering the Land of Israel.[3] In light of this, How can we invoke this episode in our prayer, using it as a basis upon which to ask Hashem to favor us in Moshe's merit?[4]

R' Meir Shapiro explains that in order to understand the inclusion of this episode in the prayer, we need to address the actual question of why Moshe deviated from Hashem's instruction and chose to hit the rock instead of speaking to it. That question itself is based on the more basic question: What was the actual difference between speaking to the rock and hitting it? Surely both were miracles! Why then did Hashem insist that Moshe do one and not the other?

Rashi explains the value of drawing water from the rock specifically through speaking to it as follows:

> *Had you spoken to the rock and it had given forth [water], I would have been sanctified before the eyes of the congregation, [for] they would have said, "If a rock that neither speaks nor hears nor has need of a livelihood fulfills the will of the Omnipresent, then all the more so should we!"*[5]

In other words, the preference of speaking to the rock over hitting it lies not in the fact that it is a higher miracle per se, but because it would have yielded an accompanying message that would inspire the people to enhance their mitzvah observance. However, this only deepens the question, for now we ask: Why would Moshe deviate from Hashem's

---

3   See *Bamidbar* 20:1–13.

4   In fact, there was an earlier episode shortly after the Jewish People left Egypt where Moshe was actually told to hit the rock and draw forth water (see *Shemos* 17:6), and some suggest that it is to that episode, where Moshe's actions were entirely in accordance with Hashem's commands, that the prayer refers. However, others point out that the prayer refers to the rock as a "*sela*," which is the term the Torah uses in the later episode of *Mei Merivah*, while in the earlier episode it is referred to as a "*tzur*."

5   *Bamidbar* 20:12, s.v. "*lehakdisheini.*"

instruction to speak to the rock, thereby foregoing the opportunity to impart a lesson to the Jewish People regarding the observance of mitzvos?

Rav Shapiro explains that the positive outcome of Moshe speaking to the rock was dependent on the spiritual level of the Jewish People on that occasion. For only if the people were on a spiritually sensitive level would they be mindful to draw the moral lesson represented by the rock responding to Hashem's word; if not, then that lesson would go unnoticed. In the latter case, far from yielding a positive result, speaking to the rock could potentially bring about a negative—even disastrous—one! For if their level is such that they do not learn the relevant lesson from the rock heeding Hashem's word, this would actually lead to an *indictment* of them for failing to heed that message!

Ultimately, the situation boiled down to Moshe's assessment of the people as he was about to bring forth water. This is the meaning of his addressing them as "מורים—rebels," prior to hitting the rock.[6] The simple meaning of the word "מורים" is teachers, not in itself a particularly negative term—unless those in question should at that time be students, in which case they will miss out on lessons that they should be learning. In light of this assessment, Moshe judged that it was better to shift toward the lower and "safer" level of miracle, and hit the rock. In other words, Moshe's decision was ultimately motivated by a desire to protect the Jewish People from potential indictment.

What emerges is that Moshe's act of hitting that rock had two aspects to it, for while the fact remains that Moshe deviated from Hashem's instructions, for which he was punished, his decision to do so was essentially motivated by *mesirus nefesh*, self-sacrifice, to protect the people. It is this second aspect of Moshe's actions that we recall at this auspicious time, asking Hashem to favor us in his merit: "For the sake of his righteousness, grant abundant water!"[7]

---

6   *Bamidbar* 20:10.

7   *Imrei Daas, Parshas Chukas*. See also *Mikraei Kodesh, Sukkos*, vol. 3, sec. 47, and responsa *Tzitz Eliezer*, vol. 17, sec. 41.

זכור פקיד שתות...רוחק מעם פחז כמים:

*Remember the appointed one [Aharon] over the Temple...
sequestered from the [Jewish] nation that is impetuous like
water.*[8]

The description of the Jewish People as "impetuous like water," requires our contemplation. First, these words were originally uttered by
Yaakov with reference to his eldest son, Reuven.[9] Where do we find that
the entire Jewish People are likewise characterized in this way?

Additionally, as we have noted, the goal of these references in this
prayer is to recall the righteousness of our forebears and to pray for
rain in their merit. In Reuven's case, the opposite was true, for it was
as a result of being impetuous like water that he forfeited his firstborn
status, as well as the institutions of priesthood and kingship![10] How,
then, is it appropriate to mention this trait when we are asking for rain?

R' Tzvi Pesach Frank explains that while the trait of impetuosity
was indeed associated with Reuven in a negative way, the context in
which it was invoked concerning the Jewish People is entirely positive.[11]
The Gemara relates that a certain heretic challenged Rava,[12] saying
that the Jewish People are an impetuous and hasty people, for when
they were offered the Torah they immediately accepted, saying "*Naaseh
Venishma*—We will do and we will hear."[13] They did not adopt a more
measured and calculated approach, first to see what was in it and then
to consider whether they wanted to accept it. To this, Rava replied
that the Jewish People's response was entirely appropriate and most
praiseworthy; since they trusted Hashem completely that whatever He

---

8   In the days leading up to Yom Kippur, the Kohen Gadol was segregated from the people
      and dwelled on the premises of the Beis Hamikdash in preparation for the special *avodah*
      on that day.

9   See *Bereishis* 49:4.

10   See *Rashi* to *Bereishis* ibid.

11   *Mikraei Kodesh*, vol. 3, sec. 49.

12   *Shabbos* 88b.

13   *Shemos* 24:7.

would command them would be for their benefit, there was no reason for them to hesitate or deliberate. Indeed, to have acted in a measured way in that situation would have been a flawed response.

In other words, when faced with a question that requires judgment, to be impetuous is a negative and costly trait. However, when presented with an offer from Hashem, that very same trait is one of extreme virtue, and it is in this regard that we refer to the Jewish People glowingly as "a nation impetuous like water." Moreover, Rav Frank adds that specifically within the context of prayer this trait is most advisable to mention. When presented with the Torah, we did not calculate, rather we instantly replied, "Hashem is our God and we are His people and so the answer is yes!" Similarly, it might conceivably be the case that we do not have sufficient merit for a good year of rain, however, invoking the concept of *middah keneged middah*, measure for measure, we ask Hashem to forego such calculations and considerations, saying rather, "They are my people and I am their God, and so the answer is yes!"

CHAPTER 22

SIMCHAS TORAH

REJOICING WITH THE TORAH–FEASTING AND DANCING

The completion of the Torah-reading cycle on Simchas Torah is accompanied by much rejoicing and celebration:

First, a celebratory feast is held in honor of completing the Torah, in the same way one is held for a regular *siyum* upon completing a *masechta*. Indeed, it appears from the early sources that the custom was to have a communal feast on this day after the service, hosted by the *Chassan Torah* and *Chassan Bereishis*.[1] In our times, when it is more common for people to eat at home, perhaps the role of celebratory feast is filled by the communal *kiddush* that many congregations have in shul. Although this may take place before the Torah reading has begun, it can perhaps be seen as a celebration in anticipation of completing the Torah. Beyond that, each person in their own home can see to it that their already festive Yom Tov meal has an added level of celebration over having completed the Torah.

Additionally, as the Torah scrolls are taken around the *bimah* during the *hakafah* circuits, we dance before them in honor of the Torah. In this, the sources encourage us to take our cue from David Hamelech

---

1   See *Tur* and *Shulchan Aruch, Orach Chaim* 669, citing *Ohr Zarua, Hilchos Sukkah*, sec. 320.

who, as the verses describe, danced with all his might before the Holy Ark when it was being taken up to Jerusalem.[2] Even though he was the king of Israel and in the presence of his subjects, he set his honor aside to give honor to the Torah, and the Torah sages throughout the generations have done likewise ever since.[3]

SYNERGY–CELEBRATION AND ELEVATION

The main objectives when it comes to the Torah are learning it and applying its teachings. As such, the celebrations on Simchas Torah upon completing the Torah reading would seem to be a break of sorts—albeit of value in themselves, and hopefully well-deserved. However, a broader perspective on the matter will show us how, while dancing with a *Sefer Torah* is not learning per se, it is not as separate from the enterprise of learning Torah as it might first appear.

The Gemara in *Berachos* makes the following rather surprising comment:

גדולה שמושה של תורה יותר מלימודה.

The serving of Torah is greater than its learning.[4]

By the "serving of Torah," the Gemara is referring to attending to the needs of a Torah sage. Needless to say, this statement requires some contemplation. After all, surely the reason the sage is deserving of being attended to is due to the Torah knowledge that he attained and possesses! If so, then why is attending to him greater than engaging in the very thing that made him great—Torah study itself?

Rav Kook explains:[5] The goal of learning Torah is to impact upon and elevate the person, and this effect will be based on two factors:

- The amount of Torah knowledge the person possesses.
- The level of regard the person has for the Torah.

---

2   See *Shmuel II* 6:14.
3   *Mishnah Berurah* 669:11.
4   7b.
5   Commentary *Ein Ayah* to *Berachos* ibid.

The crucial nature of the second element should be obvious, for if a person has abundant Torah knowledge but does not regard the Torah highly, the effect of his Torah learning will be minimal at best. Hence, the product and effect of one's Torah learning is ultimately a combination of the above two elements.

It is the nature of people's relationships with their values that when they express a value outward, it serves to embed it deeper inward. This means that if a person expresses regard for Torah, for example, by attending to a Torah scholar, that itself will instill within him all the more a regard for Torah, which will then in turn elevate *all the Torah* he learns. In this way, we can understand how, within measure, attending to Torah can be greater than learning Torah.

So too, when we come to dance with the Torah on Simchas Torah, we are giving honor to the Torah. We are raising our relationship with Torah higher, and in so doing, we are preparing and allowing ourselves to be elevated that much more by all the Torah that we have learned this past year and that we look forward to learning this coming year!

HAKAFOS ON SIMCHAS TORAH

The day of Simchas Torah is accompanied by *hakafos* around the *bimah*, just as are the days of Sukkos. However, there is a basic difference between the two:

- On Sukkos, there is a *Sefer Torah* in the middle of the circle at the *bimah*, and the people circle it holding the *arba minim*.
- On Simchas Torah, there is nothing at the *bimah*, and the people circle it holding the *Sifrei Torah*.

What is the meaning behind these two forms of *hakafos*?

Rav Yosef Dov Soloveitchik explains that whenever there is a circle, all the points along the circumference are seen as turning inward toward the center.[6] When it comes to *hakafos*, this means that whatever is at the edge of the circle represents the means through which to approach what is in the middle.

---

6   Cited in *Nefesh HaRav*, p. 221.

Therefore, on Sukkos, the *Sefer Torah* is in the middle of the circle. What is being emphasized during the *hakafos* is that Torah wisdom cannot be meaningfully acquired through intellectual investment alone. In this respect, Torah is not like other disciplines. Rather, it can only be fully absorbed when accompanied by the fulfillment of the mitzvos. As such, those who circle around the Torah circle hold the mitzvah items of the *arba minim* in their hands.

On Simchas Torah, however, the *hakafos* reflect the Gemara's teaching that in the future, Hashem will make a circle in Gan Eden with Himself in the center and place the righteous all around the circle.[7] Therefore, we do not have any physical object at the *bimah*, which is the center of our *hakafah*, for that will be occupied by the Divine Presence. Conversely, we take the Torah scrolls and circle around with them, indicating that one can only draw close to Hashem to the fullest extent possible through the study of His Torah.

There is a further element here. After all, many, if not most, of those dancing on Simchas Torah are not holding a *Sefer Torah*. With what, then, are they circling around the Divine Presence in the middle?

R' Yitzchak Isaac Sher, the Rosh Yeshiva of Slabodka, writes that the mitzvah with which most people dance on Simchas Torah is that of *"Ve'ahavta lereiacha kamocha*—You shall love your neighbor as yourself"! By joining hands with the rest of those present, they are expressing their love for their fellow Jew.[8] Through this expression of unity, not only are they celebrating their connection with the Divine Presence in the center, they are also causing it to dwell among them with greater intensity, for as the *Ramchal* writes, Hashem is One, and He connects with His people when they are one.[9]

Indeed, one may say that in a sense, on Simchas Torah we also circle the *bimah* together with the *arba minim*, just as we did on Sukkos. The only difference is that, at this stage, we are no longer holding the *arba minim*; rather, having absorbed the message of the mitzvah, we come to

---

7   *Taanis* 31a.
8   *Leket Sichos*, vol. 2, p. 136.
9   *Maamar Hachochmah.*

embody it in ourselves! The two primary themes of the *arba minim*, as highlighted in the Midrash, are as follows:

- They represent the various parts of the body—heart, spine, eyes, and mouths, which together praise Hashem.
- They represent the coming together of different types of Jews—those with Torah learning, mitzvah performance, both, or neither.[10]

So too, on Simchas Torah, all the parts of our body are enlisted when we sing and dance in honor of the Torah and Hashem. Similarly, when we dance together, all those present are included in the circle. When one chooses his place in shul, he may naturally be particular as to who should be sitting to his right and his left. However, when dancing on Simchas Torah, one takes the hand of the person on their right—whoever they might be, and gives their hand to the person on their left—whoever they might be.

And so, by taking hold of the Torah scrolls and the hands of our fellow Jews, the dancing on Simchas Torah combines the two ideas of devotion to Hashem's Torah and the love for His people—and that is a formidable and beautiful combination with which to dance before Hashem on this final day of the festival!

---

10   *Vayikra Rabbah* 30.

CHAPTER 23

THE TORAH READING ON SIMCHAS TORAH

FOUR INTRODUCTIONS–FOR BLESSINGS THAT NEED NO INTRODUCTION!

The Torah reading for Simchas Torah is, of course, the final parsha in the Torah—*Vezos Haberachah*. In light of the custom that each person gets called up to the Torah, it is common to hear the opening section of the parsha numerous times. Indeed, at a certain stage, we could probably recite many of these verses by heart. Yet our very familiarity may preclude us from asking a very simple question regarding these verses: Verse 1 seemingly introduces the blessings that Moshe gave to the people, but we don't actually hear any of them until verse 6! In between, the parsha appears to digress toward other themes: "Hashem came from Sinai...Moshe commanded us the Torah...Hashem was King among Yeshurun, etc." Important ideas, to be sure, but what are they doing wedged between the introduction of the blessings and the blessings themselves?

IN THE MIDRASH–FROM YAAKOV TO MOSHE

The commentators explain that these intervening verses actually serve as part of the introduction to Moshe's blessings. Many generations prior, after Yaakov finished blessing his sons, the verse says,

"וזאת אשר דבר להם אביהם ויברך אותם"—And this is what their father spoke to them and he blessed them."[1] Commenting on these words, the *Midrash Tanchuma* says:

"וזאת": עתיד נביא לברך אתכם כיוצא בו. במקום שפסקתי אני—הוא יברך
אתכם, וכן עשה משה שנאמר "וזאת הברכה אשר ברך משה."

"Vezos": [Yaakov said to his sons,] "In the future, a prophet will bless you similarly. In the place where I stopped, he will [commence to] bless, as it says: 'And this [Vezos] is the blessing that Moshe blessed.'"[2]

It emerges from the Midrash that Moshe's blessings were in fact a *continuation* and *completion* of Yaakov's blessings—he began where Yaakov left off!

Yet why was it necessary for Moshe to complete the blessing that Yaakov began? Why could Yaakov not give the blessing in its entirety?

The answer to this question, too, is provided by the Midrash. We have seen that the "watchword" for the transition from Yaakov's blessings to those of Moshe is "*Vezos*." The Midrash further elucidates the significance of this word:

אמר להם, אומר אני לכם אימתי מגיעות לכם הברכות האלו, משעה שתקבלו
את התורה, שנאמר "וזאת התורה אשר שם משה לפני בני ישראל."

[Yaakov] said to [his sons]: "I will tell you when these [future] blessings will be given to you, from the time that you receive the Torah, as it says, 'And this [Vezos] is the Torah that Moshe placed before the Children of Israel.'"[3]

We see that the entity that allowed for Moshe to complete Yaakov's blessings is the Torah that we received in the interim, and thus it is understood why these verses about receiving the Torah had to precede Moshe's actual blessings.

---

1   *Bereishis* 49:28.
2   Sec. 16.
3   *Devarim* 4:44.

THE BLESSINGS OF REUVEN AND YEHUDAH

A very clear illustration of this progression can be seen in the first two of Moshe's blessings—to Reuven and Yehudah. The blessings of these two tribes are very closely related to episodes where their fore-bearers erred—Reuven with Bilhah[4] and Yehudah with Tamar.[5]

- In Yaakov's blessing to Reuven, there is only criticism for his mistake, with the "blessing" being for him to take to heart the tendencies that led him to err on that occasion and to take care to avoid any such situations in the future.
- Even with Yehudah, who was praised by Yaakov for admitting his mistake and awarded the institution of kingship, there is no mention of actual atonement for his sin.

It is only when Moshe blesses these two tribes that he says, "יחי ראובן—Let Reuven live,"[6] which means, let him receive atonement for his sin,[7] and then "וזאת ליהודה—And this [atonement] should [also] be for Yehudah."[8] The basis that enabled this development was the giving of the Torah which, the Gemara informs us,[9] can achieve atonement for a person where other means prove insufficient.

Yissachar and Zevulun–Activating the Relationship

In both Yaakov and Moshe's blessings, the blessings to Zevulun and Yissachar are mentioned one after the other. However, there is one difference:

- In Yaakov's blessings, the two tribes are mentioned in two consecutive verses.[10]
- In Moshe's blessings, they are mentioned in the same verse.[11]

---

4   See *Bereishis* 35:22 with *Rashi*.
5   See *Bereishis*, chap. 38.
6   *Devarim* 33:6.
7   *Sifri*, sec. 347, cited in *Rashi, Devarim* ibid.
8   *Devarim* 33:7, *Rashi* ibid., citing the Gemara in *Makkos* 11b.
9   *Rosh Hashanah* 18a.
10 *Bereishis* 49:13–14.
11 *Devarim* 33:18.

What is behind this difference?

Rashi informs us that the relationship between these two tribes is that Zevulun engaged in commerce, thereby supporting Yissachar who were Torah scholars. As such, at the time when Yaakov gave his blessings, which was before the Torah had been given, there was not yet an actual basis for this relationship to be implemented. Therefore, Yaakov placed them "in position," but they were not actually connected at that time. With the Torah having been given in Moshe's time, their relationship could be actualized, and hence Moshe's blessing placed them both in the same verse, working together.

TORAH: THE ULTIMATE UNIFIER

An additional development that follows the giving of the Torah is expressed in the final introductory verse in our parsha:[12]

ויהי בישרון מלך בהתאסף ראשי עם יחד שבטי ישראל:

And there was a King in Yeshurun, when all the heads of the nation assembled, together the tribes of Israel.

As the verse indicates, Hashem's Presence among His people as their King is made possible by their coming together as one people, and that unity, too, is enabled by the giving of the Torah. Each tribe has its distinct character, and without a common system of Jewish living for the entire nation, they could easily become twelve separate nations. Additionally, although certain institutions pertain only to specific tribes—so that, for example, monarchy can only come from Yehudah, and priesthood from Levi—the level of Torah scholar is available to all, regardless of the particular tribe they come from. In this sense, too, the Torah allows for greater blessing, as the unity it promotes among the Jewish People brings Hashem closer to them as their King, which is the ultimate source of blessing!

This discussion can serve to give us further insight into the reading of *Parshas Vezos Haberachah* on the day of Simchas Torah. Not only

---

12   *Devarim* 33:5.

is it the final parsha of the Torah, but it also expresses the idea that the Torah is the basis for achieving higher forms of blessing. This was reflected in Moshe's blessings in his generation, and remains true for all Jews in all generations. It is well worthy of our attention on the day dedicated to celebrating our relationship with the Torah.

CHAPTER 24

CELEBRATING THE COMPLETION AND BEGINNING OF THE TORAH-READING CYCLE

WHEREFORE THE FEAST?

The day of Simchas Torah is marked by the completing of the Torah-reading cycle. Immediately upon doing so, we begin the next cycle again with the opening verses of *Chumash Bereishis*. What lies behind this practice?

The Midrash informs us that it is proper to make a celebratory feast upon completing the Torah. This is derived from Shlomo Hamelech, who was blessed by Hashem with great wisdom and understanding and, as the verse relates, upon awakening the next morning, went to Jerusalem and made a celebratory feast.[1]

Rav Yosef Dov Soloveitchik asks, What Torah did Shlomo complete that he was celebrating?[2] The verse states that he was blessed with a "wise and understanding heart,"[3] but we are not aware that had actually learned anything yet! How, then, can his actions form the basis of our

---

1   *Shir Hashirim Rabbah* 1:9.
2   *Harerei Kedem*, vol. 1, sec. 156.
3   *Melachim I* 3:12.

custom to make a feast upon completing the Torah? Rav Soloveitchik explains that from here we see that even when we celebrate the completion of the Torah, we are primarily celebrating the fact that, like Shlomo, we have received a listening and knowing heart. The joy of a *siyum* is that of anticipation for all the Torah we can now understand on a deeper level, in light of the *sefer* we have just learned.

And so, armed with the listening and understanding heart we have gained from the Torah reading we just completed, we immediately begin *Chumash Bereishis* anew, hoping to plumb its depths and receive its messages with ever greater profundity and appreciation.

SASSON AND SIMCHAH

One of the well-known lines from the *piyutim* during the *hakafos* is "שישו ושמחו בשמחת התורה—Rejoice and be happy with the joy of the Torah." According to the *Vilna Gaon*,[4] the two terms שמחה and ששון reflect two different types of joy. שמחה represents the joyous feeling of anticipation that one experiences when embarking on a meaningful venture, while ששון represents the joy that comes with the satisfaction of completing it. This distinction may be seen in the prayers on Shabbos morning, where we describe the celestial luminaries as they perform their tasks: "שמחים בצאתם וששים בבואם—Happy as they leave and joyful as they return." We see the term used in describing them as they set out is שמחים, and upon their return they are referred to as ששים.

Likewise, on Simchas Torah, our joy is twofold:

- We are joyous upon completing the present Torah-reading cycle, for which we invoke the idea of *sasson*.
- We are joyous as we embark on the new cycle, concerning which we mention the idea of *simchah*.

Indeed, it is for this reason that we say "*sisu vesimchu*," mentioning *sasson* before *simchah*, even though one surely needs to begin something

---

4   Commentary to *Iyov* 3:21.

before finishing it! However, today, we finish the Torah before beginning again, hence our *sasson* does in fact come before our *simchah*.

Chassan Torah and Chassan Bereishis

The person who is called up to the Torah for the reading of the final verses is known as the *Chassan Torah*, and the one who is called up for the opening verses of *Chumash Bereishis* is called *Chassan Bereishis*. There is a special text for the calling up of these two individuals, during which the *gabbai* says, "Amod, amod, amod [arise, arise, arise]." Why is this repeated three times, as opposed to the one time (*yaamod*) with which people are normally called up? One could say simply that this is a grand gesture to add emphasis to this special honor; however, Rav Yosef Dov Soloveitchik explains that there is a deeper meaning to this practice.[5]

The Gemara states that when one is asked to be the *sheliach tzibbur* (chazzan) for the community, he should refuse out of modesty until he is asked three times.[6] In contrast to this, when one is called up to the Torah, it is not required—or even appropriate—that he hesitate at all. The difference between the two is that being called up to the Torah purely constitutes the opportunity to perform a mitzvah, hence, there is no reason whatsoever to hesitate. By contrast, the *sheliach tzibbur* is being appointed to represent the congregation; that appointment should be accompanied by a certain sense of reservation until he is asked three times. Here too, the *Rama* writes that the final *aliyah* of the Torah should be given to the most prominent person in the community.[7] Rav Soloveitchik explains that whenever something requires the most prominent person in the community, it is because he is representing the community in that matter. Therefore, he is also called up three times, as is appropriate for appointing a *sheliach tzibbur*. The same idea is then extended to the *Chassan Bereishis*.

---

5   Cited in *Mipeninei HaRav*, p. 143.

6   *Berachos* 34a.

7   *Orach Chaim* 669, based on *Bava Basra* 15a.

THE TORAH CONTINUUM

In addition to beginning the Torah again immediately upon concluding it, there is a widespread tradition of explaining how the conclusion of *Chumash Devarim* actually leads in to the beginning of *Chumash Bereishis*. The final verse in the Torah reads:

ולכל היד החזקה ולכל המורא הגדול אשר עשה משה לעיני כל ישראל:

And for all the strong hand and for all the great awe that Moshe performed before the eyes of all Israel.

Rashi explains that the concluding words of the verse, "before the eyes of all Israel," refer to the episode of Moshe breaking the *Luchos* upon seeing the people worshipping the *Eigel Hazahav*. Why is referring to that tragic event considered the appropriate way to finish the Torah? In what way does it represent the Torah's "parting message" to the Jewish People?

R' Shlomo Zalman Auerbach explains that although the breaking of the *Luchos* was the necessary response to a catastrophic situation, it also contained a profoundly encouraging message for the Jewish People. We may ask, If the Jewish People are not worthy of receiving the *Luchos*, why break them? Why not simply return them to Heaven? The answer is that if the Jewish People do not receive the Torah, then *no other people can*, and the *Luchos* may as well be broken there and then! The destinies of the Torah and the people of Israel are exclusively intertwined with each other. By breaking the *Luchos*, Moshe was sending a message to the people: "You have made a terrible mistake, and recovery from it will not be easy; but non-recovery is not an option, for you are the only people through which the Torah will be received and through whom it will be fulfilled," and it is this very message that the Torah leaves us with at the end of *Chumash Devarim*.

The Compelling Case for Israel

Indeed, this understanding regarding the breaking of the *Luchos* can be demonstrated in a most striking way. As we know, when the Kohen

Gadol enters the Holy of Holies on Yom Kippur, he does not wear any gold. The Gemara explains that the reason for this is "אין קטיגור נעשה סניגור—The prosecution cannot become the defense."[8] In other words, gold, the material from which the *Eigel Hazahav* was made, cannot be instrumental in obtaining atonement for sins. As the Gemara outlines, this issue exists specifically within the elevated and sensitive domain of the Holy of Holies. Now, the Gemara elsewhere says that the *Aron* housed, not only the second (intact) set of *Luchos*, but also the shattered pieces of the first set.[9] How can those shattered pieces be given entry into the Holy of Holies, and what's more, into the Holy Ark? Surely there is no greater "prosecutor" than them, and they reside there the entire time!

We see from here that the enduring message of the shattered pieces is ultimately not negative at all. The message is that there can be no Torah in the world without the Jewish People. As such, not only do they not serve as a prosecution against the Jewish People; they argue for our atonement, for they embody the message that without the Jewish People, the Torah may as well be smashed into tiny pieces.

BACK TO BEREISHIS

With this in mind, we move to the beginning of *Bereishis*, where we find that this is also the opening message of the Torah.

Commenting on the opening word, *"Bereishis,"* *Rashi* writes:

אין המקרא הזה אומר אלא דרשוני, כמו שאמרו רז"ל, בשביל התורה שנקראת "ראשית דרכו," ובשביל ישראל שנקראו "ראשית תבואתה."

This verse says nothing other than "expound me." [The matter is] as our Sages, of blessed memory said, [that the Creation was] for the sake of the Torah that is called "The beginning of Hashem's way,"[10] and for the sake of Israel who are called, "the beginning [i.e., choice] of Hashem's harvest."[11]

---

8   *Rosh Hashanah* 26a.
9   *Berachos* 8b.
10 *Mishlei* 8:22.
11 *Yirmiyahu* 2:3.

This then, is what links the end of the Torah with its beginning. Neither the Torah nor the Jewish People can exist without each other in this world, and the world itself is dependent on both of them. With this in mind, we rejoice on Simchas Torah in our unique relationship with the Torah, and we embark on another year of Torah discovery—and Jewish destiny.

AFTERWORD

Carrying the Festival's Blessing Forward

At the conclusion of the middle blessing of the festival *Amidah*, we request as follows:

והשיאנו ה' אלקינו את ברכת מועדיך.

Bestow upon us, Hashem our God, the blessing of Your festival.

Each festival has a special blessing, in keeping with the unique theme of the festival itself. In this regard, the blessing of Sukkos is written explicitly in the Torah. Sukkos is *"zman simchaseinu*—the time of our joy" In *Parshas Re'eh*, the Torah concludes its discussion of Sukkos with the words "והיית אך שמח—And you shall be only happy."[1] The *Ibn Ezra* explains that this is a blessing given by the Torah.[2] Moreover, he states that the blessing is that we will have joy and happiness even beyond the festival.

On a basic level, this blessing is the Torah's reward for having celebrated Sukkos. However, on a deeper level, continued joy is a natural blessing from absorbing the themes of Sukkos over the seven days. For example:

- The special connection between Hashem and the Jewish People, and His supervision of them, as reflected by the *Ananei*

---

1   *Devarim* 16:15.
2   I.e., as opposed to denoting a mitzvah to rejoice. Commentary to *Devarim* ibid.

Hakavod. A major impediment to happiness is the anxiety over what the future will bring. When a person knows that his success is overseen and provided for from on High, from whatever source and through whatever means Hashem judges to be best for him, then as much as he continues to act diligently and responsibly, he can do so with a peaceful and happy frame of mind.

- A second impediment to happiness is craving things we do not have. When a person realizes that what he owns has been ordained from on High as what he really needs, he will find happiness with it in a way that he otherwise never would.
- Another major theme of the festival, embodied by the temporary dwelling in the sukkah, is the de-emphasizing of physical success as a primary value. This allows the person to devote their focus and drive toward more elevating goals that will bring them lasting happiness.

We do not spend the whole year in the sukkah, but how fortunate we will be if we can take the lessons we connected with over the festival and carry them forward with us into the year. They are nothing less than a recipe for happiness; keeping them in our consciousness and allowing them to inform and guide our endeavors throughout the year will make them a natural conduit for the fulfillment of the Torah's blessing, "And you shall be happy—always."

APPENDIX

Inside the Mitzvos of Sukkos

I: THE MITZVAH OF SUKKAH

INTRODUCTION: A PLACE CALLED HOME

The mitzvah of sukkah is presented in the Torah with the words, "You shall dwell in sukkos for seven days."[1] On a practical level, we know that there are certain things the halachah insists be done in the sukkah, such as having one's meals and sleeping there. However, we should not lose sight of the mitzvah as stated in the Torah. The point is not that these activities in and of themselves are the focus of the mitzvah. Rather, since they are basic staples of physical living, and are moreover activities one typically does in his own home, performing them in the sukkah asserts and establishes the sukkah as one's dwelling for these seven days, and thus serves as the base for actually dwelling there. In other words, the point is the dwelling itself, not the particular activities that help manifest it.

This will give us added insight into the special halachah that requires bread to be eaten in the sukkah on the first night of Sukkos.[2] This is a *d'Oraysa* (Torah-level) requirement that goes beyond the general

---

1   *Vayikra* 23:41.
2   See *Sukkah* 27b.

Rabbinic mitzvah of having bread at a Yom Tov meal. Since the Torah commands us to live in the sukkah for these seven days, which involves having the sukkah as our home, it is imperative to establish it as such from the outset of the festival by eating bread there.

On the converse side, the Gemara states that even after one has finished his meal on the seventh day of Sukkos, with no further plans to eat or sleep there, he should not dismantle the sukkah.[3] For the sukkah is his home for these entire seven days, and one does not dismantle one's home.[4]

LEAVING THE SUKKAH

With this idea in mind, we can understand that other activities, such as going to shul, etc., are able to be performed outside the sukkah, for as surely as one would leave his house throughout the year to go to shul, he may leave his sukkah-house to do so on Sukkos. Moreover, it is recognized and understood by all that even when one goes to shul, he is still considered to be living in his home during that time. Likewise, having established the sukkah as one's home for the festival, even when one leaves it for something one would leave home for, the sukkah remains his home at that time. This means that, on a basic level, one is still considered to be fulfilling the mitzvah of dwelling in the sukkah even while at shul![5]

INSIDE SOMEONE ELSE'S SUKKAH

In truth, there is an additional nuance in this matter, for the mitzvah goes further than requiring a person to establish the sukkah as his home during these days. After all, we know that if one visits his friend during Sukkos for a meal, he needs to eat in their sukkah. Why? Once a person has established his sukkah as his home, as surely as one might leave his *home* to eat in someone else's home, Why can he not leave his *sukkah* to eat in someone else's home? While it is true that the other

---

3   *Sukkah* 48a.

4   Commentary of the *Ran* to *Sukkah* ibid. Cf. *Rashi* ibid.

5   R' Asher Weiss, *Minchas Asher, Sukkos,* sec. 32. At the same time, when one subsequently returns to the sukkah, he will again recite the blessing of *"Leisheiv basukkah,"* over actively dwelling there, see next section.

person has their own mitzvah to make their sukkah as their home, how does that affect their visitor? And yet we see that it does, for when one eats in someone else's sukkah, he recites the blessing of "*Leisheiv basukkah*" there as well!

We see from here that the mitzvah of sukkah is not just "having *my* sukkah as *my* home," but rather, it is more generally, "having *the* sukkah as *the* home." This then applies to any home a person may visit. By placing oneself in the sukkah where one would otherwise be in the home, one is fulfilling the mitzvah of sukkah and accordingly, recite a blessing when doing so.

II: THE BLESSING OF LEISHEV BASUKKAH

TO ENTER OR TO EAT? THE GEMARA, THE POSKIM, AND THE MINHAG

The Gemara states in the name of Rabbi Yochanan that any time during the festival that one enters the sukkah after not having been there for a significant amount of time, one recites the blessing of "*Leisheiv basukkah*."[6] A simple reading of this ruling would seem to indicate that the blessing is recited simply over entering and being in the sukkah, regardless of what one does there. Indeed, this is how the halachah is codified by the *Rif*[7] and the *Rambam*.[8] However, numerous Rishonim cite the position of Rabbeinu Tam, who states that the blessing is specifically recited when one has a meal in the sukkah.[9] Both the *Shulchan Aruch* and the *Rama* record that the accepted practice (*minhag*) is in accordance with the opinion of Rabbeinu Tam.[10]

It should be emphasized that Rabbeinu Tam does not mean to say that the blessing is recited over the act of eating per se. Rather, having a meal represents the dwelling in the sukkah as a whole and, as such, it serves as an anchor for the blessing over all aspects of the mitzvah.

---

6   *Sukkah* 45b.
7   Ibid.
8   *Hilchos Sukkah* 6:12.
9   See, for example, *Rosh, Sukkah* 4:3 and *Mordechai* ibid., sec. 765.
10   *Orach Chaim* 639:8.

What type of meal necessitates this blessing? In general, the food that assumes primary significance with regard to eating is bread. As such, it would seem that the blessing would only be recited when one has a meal that includes bread. At the same time, there exists a concept whereby if one partakes of baked goods whose blessing is *Mezonos* to the extent that this constitutes his meal (as opposed to a snack), this is also considered a significant meal.[11] Accordingly, the *Shulchan Aruch* rules that if one has *Mezonos* foods as a meal, he should recite the blessing of *Leisheiv basukkah*.[12]

However, the *Mishnah Berurah* cites a widespread custom of people reciting the blessing when eating anything more than an egg-volume of *Mezonos* food, which is the amount that it is forbidden to eat outside of the sukkah.[13] The *Mishnah Berurah* is somewhat concerned over what appears to be a custom to recite a blessing unnecessarily. However, he does not negate the custom. Rather, he recommends staying in the sukkah for a while afterward so that the blessing also covers the time he spends in the sukkah.

Thus, we see the prominence and influence of *minhag* regarding when to recite the blessing over the sukkah, both initially, in terms of siding with Rabbeinu Tam that the blessing is recited specifically before eating, and later on, in terms of defining what type of eating requires a blessing.

III: RECITING THE BLESSING OVER THE ARBA MINIM

INTRODUCTION: A HALACHIC CATCH-22

The common practice when reciting the blessing over the *arba minim* is to take all four species in hand with the *esrog* upside down, recite the

---

11 Indeed, the halachah regarding one who eats *Mezonos* baked goods as a meal is that he recites the blessing of *Hamotzi* before eating and *Birkas Hamazon* afterward, as he would for actual bread.

12 Ibid., *se'if* 2.

13 Ibid., sec. 16.

blessing, and then turn the *esrog* the right way up and wave the *arba minim*. The background to this practice is discussed in *Tosafos*,[14] and is based on taking three halachic points into consideration:

- The blessing over a mitzvah has to be recited prior to the performance of that mitzvah.
- The item with which one fulfills the mitzvah should be in one's hand at the time of the blessing.
- As soon as one has picked up the *arba minim*, he has fulfilled the mitzvah on its most basic level.

As we can appreciate, it is impossible to recite the blessing in a straightforward manner in a way that will satisfy all the above concerns. One cannot have the *arba minim* in hand when reciting the blessing and also fulfill the idea of reciting the blessing before the performing the mitzvah, for as soon as he has picked them up, the mitzvah has already been fulfilled, leaving him "post-mitzvah" before he can make the blessing! For this reason, *Tosafos* recommend initially holding the *esrog* upside down. Since the mitzvah cannot be fulfilled until one holds all the species the right way up, he is thus able to have them all in hand and recite the blessing before then turning the *esrog* the right way up and fulfilling the mitzvah.

Interestingly, this method (Option A) is actually one of three mentioned in *Tosafos*:

- Option A: Pick up all four species, but hold the *esrog* upside down until after reciting the blessing.
- Option B: Pick up three of the species (the *lulav* together with the *hadasim* and *aravos*), make the blessing, and then pick up the *esrog*.
- Option C: Pick up all four species the right way up, but with express intention not to fulfill the mitzvah until after reciting the blessing, for a person cannot fulfill a mitzvah if he does not wish to do so. Therefore, he can have all the species in hand and still recite the blessing prior to fulfilling the mitzvah.

---

14   *Sukkah* 39a, s.v. *"oveir."*

The Mitzvah–To Raise Up or to Take Hold?

We have stated that the basic mitzvah is fulfilled by picking up the *arba minim*. This understanding would seem to be supported by the expression of the Gemara concerning them, "מדאגביה נפק ליה—Once he has lifted it [the *lulav*] up, he has fulfilled his obligation."[15] Indeed, according to some, this idea is indicated by the formula of the blessing we recite. The Torah commands us in the mitzvah of *arba minim* by saying, "ולקחתם לכם—You shall take for yourselves," yet, as we know, in the blessing we say "על נטילת לולב." Why do we diverge from the term used by the Torah? Why do we not say "*Al lekichas lulav*"? The word "נטילה" means taking, but it also means lifting up. Therefore, we use this term in the blessing, which includes the idea that the *arba minim* need to be lifted up in order to fulfill the mitzvah.[16]

There are other authorities, however, who maintain that one can fulfill the basic mitzvah simply by taking the *arba minim* in hand without raising them up, as indicated by the words of the verse, "ולקחתם לכם—You shall take for yourselves." Indeed, this would appear to be the position of *Tosafos*, cited above. For if *Tosafos* understand that one needs to raise the *arba minim* up in order to fulfill the mitzvah, why do they not simply recommend regarding the blessing that one take the species in hand, make the blessing, and then raise them up? Rather, it is apparent that they concur that taking the species in hand already suffices to fulfill the mitzvah; hence, they needed to come up with other possibilities in order to recite the blessing with the species in hand but before fulfilling the mitzvah.[17]

---

15   *Sukkah* 42a.

16   R' Shlomo HaKohen of Vilna, responsa *Binyan Shlomo* 1:48.

17   *Rashash, Sukkah* 42a. Yet a third approach maintains that the basic mitzvah is fulfilled by merely having the species in hand, even without taking them (*Netziv*, responsa *Meishiv Davar* 1:40). A practical difference between this approach and the earlier ones would occur on the first day of Sukkos where one is required to own the species with which one fulfills the mitzvah. If one does not have his own *arba minim*, he will need to first acquire them from someone else by lifting them up. Yet, at this stage, when he wishes to now fulfill the mitzvah, he will first have to put them down and then pick them up again, since when he first took hold of them, they were not his. According to the third opinion, this would not be necessary, since he is only required to have them in hand, which he does as soon as he acquires them (R' Yaakov Ettlinger, *Bikkurei Yaakov* 652:19).

THE SHULCHAN ARUCH'S CHOICES

Of the three options presented by *Tosafos* as to how to recite the blessing, only the first two are mentioned in the *Shulchan Aruch*.[18] It would seem that the reason for this is that the *Shulchan Aruch* wanted to present the approaches that would work best for everyone, hence, he chose those which involve practical steps, such as taking only three of the species or holding the *esrog* upside down. The third approach is much more subtle, relying on the person having the intention not to fulfill the mitzvah when he picks up the species until after he has recited the blessing. Ensuring that this intention is in place is more demanding than the other approaches, for it is very easy to simply pick up the species without thinking about it one way or the other. Therefore, the *Shulchan Aruch* chose the two other more "user-friendly" approaches.[19]

The only proviso to bear in mind regarding the prevalent approach of holding the *esrog* upside down during the blessing is that one should ensure to hold it that way *from the time he picks it up*! If a person assumes this approach but is not aware of its background, he could quite naturally first pick up the *esrog* the right way up, and then turn it upside down for the blessing before turning it the right way up again, thereby forfeiting the benefit of this practice in the first place.[20]

We may ask further: If the mitzvah is to take hold of the species, then if one follows the approach of initially taking the *esrog* upside down, when he subsequently turns it the right way up, it is already in his hand, so where is the "taking" through which he fulfills the mitzvah with the *esrog*? The commentators explain that here, the act of turning the *esrog* the right way up is considered a new act of taking through which he now fulfills the mitzvah (*Mikraei Kodesh*, vol. 2, sec. 3, fn. 2.)

18   *Orach Chaim* 651:5.

19   By contrast, the *Vilna Gaon* (commentary to *Hilchos Lulav* ibid.) favors the final approach of "negative intention."

20   Indeed, it is out of concern for this mistake that the *Aruch Hashulchan* favors the other approach mentioned in the *Shulchan Aruch*, namely, reciting the blessing while holding the *lulav* but before taking the *esrog*.

IV: HIDUR MITZVAH AND ARBA MINIM

TWO APPLICATIONS OF HIDUR MITZVAH

As we have seen, the general concept of *hidur mitzvah* (beautifying a mitzvah) is derived from the verse "זה א-ל-י ואנוהו—This is my God and I will glorify Him,"[21] which is expounded by the Sages to mean "I will beautify the mitzvos before Him."[22] Within the mitzvah of *arba minim*, *hidur mitzvah* finds expression in two ways:

- **Appearance**: The Mishnayos in the third *perek* of *Maseches Sukkah* state that any of the *arba minim* that are dry or otherwise fundamentally lacking in *hidur* are disqualified for the mitzvah. *Tosafos* explain that although a lack of *hidur* does not generally disqualify the mitzvah object,[23] here, the Torah itself refers to the *esrog* as a "*pri eitz hadar*," a beautiful fruit.[24] This indicates that when it comes to the *esrog*—and, by extension, the other three species—the requirement of *hidur* is much more of the essence, and its absence can render the item categorically unfit.
- **Binding the species together**: The Gemara states that although the species do not need to be bound together in order to fulfill the mitzvah, nevertheless, we do so as a *hidur mitzvah*.[25] In this instance, the Gemara explicitly mentions the verse "*Zeh Keili ve'anveihu*."

With regard to this second aspect, the *Shulchan Aruch* rules that the species should be bound together specifically with a double-knot, and not, for example with a bow, which is less permanent.[26] Some commentators find difficulty with this ruling. After all, a plain double-knot does

---

21   *Shemos* 15:3.
22   *Shabbos* 133b.
23   *Sukkah* 29b, s.v. "*lulav*."
24   *Vayikra* 23:39.
25   *Sukkah* 11b.
26   *Orach Chaim* 651:1. (A common means through which the species are bound together is by the holder made from palm leaves known as a *koishikel*. The *Mishnah Berurah* [ibid.] explains that this arrangement is also considered the equivalent of a double-knot.)

not beautify the *lulav* bundle more than would a bow. If anything, a bow looks nicer! As such, what lies behind the *Shulchan Aruch*'s insistence on a double-knot, specifically?

OBJECTS AND ACTIONS

The *Avnei Nezer* of Sochatchov explains that there are two elements to consider within a mitzvah:[27]

- The object with which one performs the mitzvah
- The action of performing the mitzvah

Having noted these two elements, it is important to realize that *hidur mitzvah* applies to both; as surely as it is relevant regarding the area of beautifying the mitzvah object, it is likewise relevant when it comes to beautifying the action through which one performs the mitzvah. An illustration of this second type of *hidur* can be seen in a statement of *Tosafos*,[28] who say that even though there are certain speech-related mitzvos where a person can fulfill his obligation through listening to someone else, nevertheless, if possible, the person should fulfill the mitzvah himself as a *hidur mitzvah*. In that case, the "object" of the mitzvah, i.e., the words, do not necessarily come out more beautifully when he says them; rather, the *hidur* lies purely in the realm of action, i.e., of the person being particular to perform the mitzvah himself.

In light of the above, the *Avnei Nezer* proceeds to explain that when it comes to the mitzvah of *arba minim*, the two types of *hidur* we have discussed relate to these two areas, respectively. On the one hand, the requirement that the species not be dry or impaired clearly relates to the *hidur* of the object. However, the idea of binding the species to-gether is not to make them look nicer. Rather, since the species should ideally be taken together, binding them with each other makes them more "together," and is thereby an enhancement of the action of taking them together. As such, the *Shulchan Aruch* rules that they should be bound together with a double-knot. For, even though a bow might look

---

27   Responsa *Orach Chaim* 433.
28   *Berachos* 21b, s.v. "*ad.*"

nicer, the focus here is not the enhanced appearance of the object, but the enhanced quality of the action, and a double-knot is more effective in that regard than a bow. Indeed, this understanding can be perceived clearly within *Rashi's* words in explaining the mitzvah of binding the species together: "They should be bound together in order that they can be taken together."[29]

V: NAANUIM

As is well known, the way the mitzvah of *arba minim* is performed is by holding the species together and waving them in all four directions and up and down. This waving is known as *naanuim*. Where does it come from? As we noted above, the Gemara explicitly states that one has fulfilled the mitzvah simply by picking the species up. In light of this, what role do the *naanuim* play in a mitzvah that one has already fulfilled?

R' Yerucham Fischel Perlow explains the matter as follows:[30] The Mishnah informs us that in the Beis Hamikdash, the Torah-level mitzvah of *arba minim* applies all seven days of Sukkos,[31] while everywhere else it applies only on the first day, as the verse says "You shall take for yourselves on the first day, etc."[32] And indeed, in the times of the Beis Hamikdash, in all locations other than the Beis Hamikdash, the *arba minim* were only taken on the first day. However, after the Beis Hamikdash was destroyed, Rabbi Yochanan ben Zakkai instituted that the *arba minim* be taken for seven days in all locations as a *zecher laMikdash* (remembrance of the Beis Hamikdash), and this remains our practice today until the Beis Hamikdash is rebuilt. Regarding this matter, two questions arise:

- What is the source of the idea that the mitzvah of *lulav* applies for seven days in the Beis Hamikdash?

---

29 *Sukkah* 37b, s.v. *"dilma."*
30 Commentary to *Sefer Hamitzvos* of Rav Saadya Gaon, endnotes to vol. 3, sec. 5.
31 *Sukkah* 41a.
32 *Vayikra* 23:39.

- What is the relationship between the seven-day mitzvah in the Beis Hamikdash and the one-day mitzvah everywhere else? Are they essentially the same mitzvah with just a difference in duration between the two places, or are they actually two separate mitzvos?

Rav Perlow explains that when we answer the first question, we will have the answer to the second. As we have mentioned, the source for taking the *lulav* on the first day are the words, "You shall take for yourselves, etc." The source for the mitzvah in the Beis Hamikdash is the second half of that verse, which reads, "And you shall rejoice before Hashem, your God, for seven days." The Sages explain that this "rejoicing before Hashem," i.e., in the Beis Hamikdash, takes the form of the mitzvah of *arba minim* during all seven days of Sukkos.

Having seen the sources for these two mitzvos, we can now proceed to discern the difference in nature between them. The general mitzvah on the first day, which derives from "You shall take," is fulfilled by just that—taking the species. But what about the mitzvah in the Beis Hamikdash, which is learned from "you shall rejoice"? How is that mitzvah fulfilled?

The answer is, through *naanuim*!

The *naanuim* with the *arba minim* are the celebratory waving through which we express our joy before Hashem. In our own experience, we know that celebrations are often accompanied by the waving of flags and banners, etc. In fact, there is precedent for this idea in the Tanach as well. *Shmuel II* relates how the *Aron* (Holy Ark) was brought up to Yerushalayim. In describing the celebratory procession, it states: "David and the entire House of Israel were rejoicing before Hashem with all manner of wood-instruments, with harps, lyres...*and with waving objects* [*menaane'im*]."[33] We see that this celebration was accompanied by and expressed through waving objects. Moreover, commenting on this verse, the Midrash states that these *menaane'im* were none other than *lulavim*![34]

---

33 *Shmuel II* 6:5.
34 *Bamidbar Rabbah* 4:20.

What emerges from the above is that the *naanuim* only exist as part of the mitzvah of "you shall rejoice" in the Beis Hamikdash but have no role within the mitzvah of "you shall take" in other locations. The reason we all perform the mitzvah with *naanuim* is because when Rabbi Yochanan ben Zakkai instituted the mitzvah for seven days as a remembrance of the *Mikdash*, he instituted that it be performed *as it was in the Mikdash*, i.e., with *naanuim*![35]

In a similar—although slightly more moderate—vein, R' Leib Mintzberg explains that although the Torah only *commands* us to rejoice with the *arba minim* in the Beis Hamikdash, the fact that it commands us to take the very same species outside the Beis Hamikdash indicates that this too is part of that rejoicing in an extended sense.[36] The very taking of the species in hand celebrates our relationship with Hashem, the gift of the Land of Israel, and the harvest we have been blessed with therein. Thus, it stands to reason that even in the absence of a command to do so outside of the Beis Hamikdash, to wave the species constitutes the full fulfillment of the mitzvah, or, as the *Rambam* refers to it, "*mitzvah kehilchesah*—the mitzvah as it should ideally be performed."

At any rate, we see that the *naanuim* are an integral part of the way in which the mitzvah is performed. The halachic ramifications of this idea are expressed by the *Mishnah Berurah*.[37] Although the common practice is not to hold all the *arba minim* the right way up prior to reciting the blessing so it can be recited before fulfilling the mitzvah,[38] nevertheless, if a person forgot and took them all the right way up, he still recites the blessing! For since he has not yet waved them, he is still considered to be at a stage prior to the complete fulfillment of the mitzvah, and hence is still able to recite the blessing.[39]

---

35   Rav Perlow adds that this is true even on the first day when taking the *lulav* is a Torah mitzvah in all locations, so that the performance of the mitzvah on the first day should not involve less than on subsequent days.

36   *Ben Melech, Sukkos, maamar* 4.

37   651:24, citing *Magen Avraham* and *Pri Megadim*. The origins of this ruling are also in *Tosafos*.

38   See above, section 3.

39   However, from the fact that *Tosafos* make other recommendations regarding how to recite the blessing before holding all four species, it is clear that in their opinion, the basic mitzvah

Additionally, the halachah states that while the minimum length for *hadasim* and *aravos* is three *tefachim* (handbreadths), the *lulav* requires at least four. The Gemara explains that the reason for this extra *tefach* is in order to be able to wave with it, for the waving is fulfilled primarily with the *lulav*. We see from here that even though a person can fulfill the mitzvah without waving the *lulav*, nevertheless, if the *lulav* is not at least *in principle* fit to be waved, it is disqualified *even for the basic mitzvah!*

Indeed, Rav Yosef Dov Soloveitchik explains that it is for this reason the blessing over the *arba minim* mentions the *lulav* specifically ("*al netilas lulav*"). Since it is through the *lulav* that one can fulfill the mitzvah in its optimum way, i.e., through *naanuim*, it receives distinct mention and indeed, represents all the other species in the blessing that we recite.

VI: HOSHANOS

Every day during Sukkos, there is a section of the prayers called *Hoshanos*, where we circle the *bimah* while holding the *arba minim* and recite special prayers. This is based on the practice during the time of the Beis Hamikdash where the Kohanim would circle the *Mizbeiach* each day. As we discussed, the circuits around the *Mizbeiach* are, in essence, a parade that embodies the idea of "rejoicing before Hashem" during Sukkos.[40] Hence, the halachah states that if a person is unfortunately in a time of mourning, they do not participate in the *Hoshanos* circuit.[41]

In this regard, there is room to raise a further question. Sukkos is a time of joy and celebration of Hashem's goodness in general, yet we have also seen that the mitzvah to rejoice "before Hashem" takes the specific form of waving the *arba minim* during all seven days of Sukkos. As such, when we say that the *Hoshanos* are a fulfillment of "rejoicing before Hashem" on Sukkos, this can be understood in one of two ways:

- It is possible to see the *hakafos* simply as a separate mitzvah expressing the joy of Sukkos alongside that of the *arba minim*.

---

is fulfilled by simply taking the species together, even on the days where the mitzvah exists as a remembrance of the Mikdash.

40   See chapter 13, "*Hoshanos*."

41   *Rama, Orach Chaim* 660:2, with commentary of the *Vilna Gaon* ibid.

- It is also possible to see them as an *enhanced fulfillment* of the mitzvah of *arba minim*. As we have seen, the basic mitzvah of *arba minim* is fulfilled simply by taking hold of them. Beyond that, we saw that the mitzvah of rejoicing with the *arba minim* takes the form of the *naanuim* wavings. To this end, the *Hoshanos* represent a further level still of not only holding and waving the *arba minim*, but also of parading with them!

Is there any way to discover which of the two above approaches is represented by the *Hoshanos*?

R' Leib Mintzberg[42] states that the understanding of the nature of the *hakafos* can be demonstrated by the ruling of the *Rama*,[43] who says that if a person does not have a set of *arba minim*, they do not participate in the *hakafah* circuits. Why should not having *arba minim* exclude them from this part of the prayers? We see from here that the *hakafos* during *Hoshanos* are essentially an extension of the mitzvah of *arba minim*; hence, there is no purpose in circling the *bimah* if one doesn't have the species in hand.[44]

This idea can also explain why we accompany the circuits with the recitations of *Hoshanos*, which are prayers for salvation. We mentioned in an earlier chapter that the reason we wave the *lulav* when we say "אנא ה' הושיע נא—Please Hashem save now" during *Hallel* is because the waving of the *lulav* is in the category of "*sheyarei mitzvah*," an additional enhancing measure within the mitzvah. The Gemara states that such additional practices have the quality of warding off calamity;[45] hence, we wave the *lulav* when we ask Hashem to save us, for we are saying, in the merit of practices such as waving the *lulav*, save us! Accordingly, once we appreciate that the *hakafah* circuits are a further enhancing

---

42 *Ben Melech, Sukkos, maamar 7.*

43 *Orach Chaim* 660:2.

44 The *Shulchan Aruch* himself rules that even one who does not have *arba minim* circuits the *bimah*. Apparently, he adopts the second understanding of *Hoshanos*, whereby they are a separate mitzvah of expressing the joy of the festival (*Ben Melech* ibid.).

45 *Sukkah* 37b.

measure, we will understand why they, too, are accompanied by prayers for salvation from any mishap or misfortune.[46]

VII: NISUCH HAMAYIM

One of the unique *korbanos* of Sukkos is the *nisuch hamayim*—water libation. Although wine libations are offered on the *Mizbeiach* on every day of the year, water is offered only on Sukkos.

A basic question arises regarding the fundamental nature of this special *korban*. The background to this question is that *nesachim* can come in two forms:

- As an attachment to an animal *korban* that is being offered
- As an independent and self-contained offering

In light of this, it is worthwhile contemplating the designation of the water libation on Sukkos:

- Is it an independent *korban* as its own mitzvah during these days?
- Or is it perhaps attached to one of the animals that are offered as a *korban* during the festival?

This question is not purely conceptual in nature, for in principle, it could also have practical ramifications. For example, the halachah states that a *nesech* that is brought by itself can be offered even at night, while a *nesech* that accompanies a *korban* can be offered only during the day, just as is the law with the *korban* itself.[47] As such, if the water libation was brought during nighttime, has the obligation been fulfilled? If it is a separate obligation, then the mitzvah would be fulfilled, but if it an attachment to a *korban*, then it would not.

Alternatively, if it were ever to be the case that there were no animals available to offer as *korbanos* during Sukkos, Would there still be a mitzvah to perform *nisuch hamayim*? Here, too, the answer would

---

46   *Ben Melech* ibid.
47   See *Menachos* 44b.

depend on our understanding of the nature of the *nesech*. If it is an independent mitzvah, then there would be no reason not to bring it by itself. However, if it is an attachment to the *korbanos*, then in the absence of the *korbanos* themselves there would be no reason to offer the water.

In this regard, it is worth noting that the *Talmud Yerushalmi* rules that if the water was offered at night, the mitzvah has been fulfilled.[48] In other words, the *Yerushalmi* views *nisuch hamayim* as a separate obligation of the festival and not as an attachment to one of the *korbanos*.[49]

Taking the matter one stage further, R' Chaim Soloveitchik of Brisk explains that the question of how to understand the nature of *nisuch hamayim* will depend of the source in the Torah from where it is derived.[50] The Gemara in *Sukkah* states that *nisuch hamayim* is a *"halachah l'Moshe miSinai,"* a law that was communicated orally by Hashem to Moshe and is not based on a verse.[51] Elsewhere, however, the Gemara records the opinions of three Tannaim who derive the mitzvah of *nisuch hamayim* from sources in the Torah:

- **Rabbi Yehudah ben Beseira**: In the parsha of the *mussaf* offerings for Sukkos, there are three extra letters, *mem, yud,* and *mem*, which spell the word *mayim*—water.
- **Rabbi Akiva**: In the verse regarding the sixth day, the word "ונסכיה—its libations" is used in the plural form, denoting not only the regular libation of wine, but also the special libation of water.
- **Rabbi Nosson**: In chapter 28 of *Bamidbar*, the verse uses the double expression regarding *nesachim* "נסך נסך," denoting the two kinds of *nesech*, namely, of wine and of water.[52]

---

48   This is also codified by the *Rambam* (*Hilchos Temidim* 10:7).
49   See commentary of the *Ritva* to *Sukkah* 50a. See also *Meshech Chochmah* to *Bamidbar* 29:17–18.
50   Cited in *Chiddushei HaGriz* to *Menachos* 15b.
51   48a.
52   *Taanis* 2b.

When we consider these three sources, we will notice something very interesting:

- In Rabbi Akiva's source, the plural term "its libations" is stated with reference to the morning *tamid* offering, for the verse states that the *mussaf* offering should be "aside from the daily burnt offering...and its libations." This indicates that both the wine and the water libations that are offered on Sukkos belong to the *tamid* offering.
- In Rabbi Nosson's source, the double expression "הסך נסך," is actually written in the parsha dealing with the *tamid* offering. This, too, clearly implies that both of those *nesachim* are accompaniments to the *tamid*.
- In Rabbi Yehudah ben Beseira's source, of the three extra letters that form the word "מים," two of them are also written in words that relate to the *tamid* offering.

On the other hand, the opinion that sees the *nisuch* as coming from a *halachah l'Moshe miSinai*, a pure oral transmission, can see it as separate *nesech* obligation.

Thus, it emerges that the question of the source for *nisuch hamyaim* relates not just to its origins, but also to its conceptual definition.

GLOSSARY

Acharonim: later commentators.

Akeidah: the binding of Yitzchak.

aliyah: being called up to the Torah.

amah (pl. amos): cubit.

Amidah: standing prayer.

aravah (pl. aravos): willow, one of the four species.

Ananei Hakavod: the Clouds of Glory.

arba minim: the four species.

Aseres Yemei Teshuvah: the Ten Days of Repentance (from Rosh Hashanah to Yom Kippur).

avodah: Divine service.

Beis Hamikdash: the Holy Temple.

bimah: the table in the middle of the synagogue upon which the Torah is read.

Birkas Hamazon: Grace After Meals.

bitachon: trust in Hashem.

Bnei Yisrael: the Children of Israel.

Chassan Bereishis: honoree called to the Torah for the beginning of *Parshas Bereishis* on Simchas Torah.

Chassan Torah: honoree called to the Torah for the completion of *Parshas Vezos Haberachah* on Simchas Torah.

chatas: sin offering.

Cheit Ha'eigel: Sin of the Golden Calf

Chol Hamoed: the intermediate days of Sukkos.

David Hamelech: King David.

d'Oraysa: Torah law.

esrog: citron, one of the four species.

Gan Eden: the Garden of Eden.

hadas (pl. hadasim): myrtle, one of the four species.

hakafah (pl. hakafos): circuit around the bimah.

halachah: the body of Torah law.

Har Sinai: Mount Sinai.

hidur: beautification.

hishtadlus: investing effort.

Hoshana Rabbah: the seventh day of Sukkos.

Hoshanos: prayers recited on Sukkos while circling the bimah.

Kohanim: Priests.

Koheles: the Book of Ecclesiastes.

Kohen Gadol: High Priest.

korban (pl. korbanos): offering.

Luchos: the two tablets of stone upon which the Ten Commandments were engraved.

lulav: palm branch, one of the four species.

Maseches: tractate of the Talmud.

mesirus nefesh: self-sacrifice.

midbar: wilderness.

Midrash: collection of Aggadic teachings from the Sages.

minhag: custom.

Mishkan: Tabernacle.

Mishnah (pl. Mishnayos): the compilation of the Oral Law.

mitzvah (pl. mitzvos): a commandment.

Mizbeiach: Altar.

moed (pl. moadim): festival.

naanuim: waving of the four species.

mussaf: additional offerings for Shabbos and festivals.

nesech (pl. nesachim): libation offered on the Mizbeiach.

nisuch hamayim: water libation offered on Sukkos.

poskim: halachic authorities.

Pirkei Avos: the tractate of Mishnah that deals with Jewish ethics and outlook.

piyut (pl. piyutim): liturgical poem.

pshat: straightforward meaning.

Rishonim: early commentators.

schach: covering of the sukkah.

Shalosh Regalim: the three festivals of Pesach, Shavuos, and Sukkos.

Shem Adnus: the name referring to Hashem as Master of the world.

Shem Havayah: the special four-letter name of Hashem, known as the Tetragrammaton.

Shlomo Hamelech: King Solomon.

shul: synagogue.

simchah: joy.

Simchas Beis Hashoeivah: the celebration around the drawing of the water on Sukkos.

siyum: celebration upon completing a tractate of Talmud.

sukkah: (1) temporary abode in which we dwell during Sukkos, (2) the tractate of Mishnah that deals with the laws of Sukkos.

tamid: daily offering.

Tanach: acronym for Torah, Neviim, and Kesuvim; the Bible.

Tannaim: rabbis of the Mishnah.

techiyas hameisim: revival of the dead.

Tehillim: the book of Psalms.

teshuvah: repentance.

Tishrei: the first month in the Hebrew year.

todah: thanksgiving offering.

Ushpizin: the seven illustrious guests who visit the sukkah on each day of Sukkos.

Yamim Noraim: Days of Awe (Rosh Hashanah and Yom Kippur).

Yom Tov: festival.

ABOUT THE AUTHOR

Born and raised in London, Rabbi Immanuel Bernstein learned in Yeshivas Ateres Yisrael, Jerusalem, and received his rabbinic ordination from Rabbi Chaim Walkin. Rabbi Bernstein currently teaches in Yeshivas Machon Yaakov, Jerusalem, as well as in various seminaries, and gives a popular weekly *shiur* on Chumash that is open to the public and available online. He is the author of seven books, *Teshuvah: A Guide for the Heart and Mind during Elul, Rosh Hashanah, and Yom Kippur*; *Aggadah: Sages, Stories and Secrets*; *Darkness to Destiny: The Haggadah Experience*; *Purim: Removing the Mask*; *The Call of Sinai: A Deeper Look at Torah, the Omer, and the Festival of Shavuos*; *Chanukah: Capturing the Light*; and *Dimensions in Chumash* (Mosaica Press). He lives in Jerusalem with his family. Visit Rabbi Bernstein at www.journeysintorah.com.

In loving memory of

R' SHLOMO HENICH MENDELOWITZ

הר"ר שלמה העניך בן ר' שמואל זאב

Upright and beloved by all, a symbol of loving kindness,
who raised his children to love Torah and mitzvos

ת.נ.צ.ב.ה.

In honor of

ILYA BRATSLAVSKY

אליהו בן מרדכי

ת.נ.צ.ב.ה.